World's Tallest Woman:

The Giantess of Shelbyville High

A novel based on the real-life experiences of
Sandy Allen

Rita Rose

Hawthorne Publishing
Carmel, Indiana 46033
www.hawthornepub.com

First printing, 2008

ISBN: 978-0-9787167-9-0   (Hardcover)
          978-0-9726273-3-7   (Softcover)

Though this book follows the life experiences of Sandy Allen, and though she reviewed this book and believed it portrayed a part of her life accurately, this is a work of fiction.

Cover photo by *The Indianapolis Star* is of Sandy with Annie Hopper.

Printed in the United States of America

Sandy Allen, Class of 1973,
Shelbyville High School, home of the beloved Golden Bears.
Here's to you, girl!

1

Roseann Bellamy paused outside the door of the Shelbyville High School office and stared at her schedule of classes. World history was first, her worst subject. It figures, she sighed. Roseann adjusted her books, then hurried across the Student Center to the stairway.

"Hey!" someone yelled. "You a senior?"

The voice seemed to be directed at Roseann, who whirled around and nearly lost her balance. She was face-to-face with a gum-cracking girl with bleached blond hair who was wearing a black mini-skirt.

"You a senior?" the girl repeated, putting a hand on her hip.

"Junior," Roseann said, slightly flustered.

"Only seniors are allowed to walk on the school emblem," the girl said flatly, pointing to Roseann's feet. Roseann looked down: She was standing on the likeness of a bear wearing a black and gold sweater with the school logo on the front. The school team—the Golden Bears—flashed through her mind.

"Sorry," Roseann said. How was she supposed to know? "I'm new here."

Two boys walked by and stared. "Wow, Lisa nailed a redhead," one of them said, poking the other boy on the arm with his knuckles. Roseann's face grew hot.

"Well," said the girl they were calling Lisa, narrowing her blue-shadowed eyes at Roseann, "now you know." She turned on her heel and started to walk away.

Roseann stood there for a moment, feeling angry and helpless. "Well excuuuuuse me!" she finally shouted after the girl. She turned toward the stairway and continued on to her first class.

Great, she thought. My first five minutes in this school and I've already committed the sin of walking on the stupid bear in the Student Center. She was afraid to think about what the rest of the day would be like.

The history classroom was bustling with kids in high spirits, laughing and greeting each other after summer vacation. Roseann didn't know any of them since she had just moved to Shelbyville a month ago. She maneuvered around a cluster of girls near the doorway and found a seat in the back of the room where she hoped she would be inconspicuous.

I am a total freak in this awful school, she thought bitterly.

Shelbyville High School. Even the name turned her off. Thirty miles from my hometown and I'm in a foreign country, Roseann grumbled to herself.

She wished her father had never taken a new job as director of financial affairs at Shelbyville Hospital. For one thing, he was hardly ever home anymore. Roseann felt a pang of regret over her selfishness: She knew it was a great financial move for her family. Jack Bellamy's salary had jumped considerably, enabling her mom to quit work and stay home more with Scott, the nine-year-old hyperactive brother who drove her crazy most of the time.

But Shelbyville! Surely there were more interesting places to find a job. Why not in a big city like Indianapolis, where she was born and raised? There were hospitals there, too.

Roseann thought that Shelbyville was the most boring town on the map and that its only high school has to be one step above the Dark Ages. How could she become a famous writer in farm country? "This is the 70s!" she had said to her mother just that morning. "There isn't even a morning paper. How do people live like this?'"

The history teacher, Mr. Wallace, attempted to bring the room to order. He was a skinny, dark-haired man with a leering expression. He selected two students from the front row to pass out textbooks, a task which promised to take a while. Roseann flipped open a spiral notebook, unclipped the pen attached to the inside cover and started a letter to Ashley Stevens, her best friend in Indianapolis.

"Ash," she wrote without any preliminary greeting, "this place SUCKS."

So far, Ashley had only sent her a short note tucked in a Congratulations On Your New Home card, which Roseann promptly tossed aside. None of her other friends had written either. Only a month here and already her old friends had forgotten about her. So had her boyfriend, she thought, tears stinging her eyes.

"I'll write," Kyle had promised her on the day she left the city. He never had.

Someone plopped a large textbook on Roseann's desk, interrupting her thoughts. She shut her notebook and stared at the history text, sarcastically wondering if there was a picture of Shelbyville High inside that said "Country schoolhouse in ancient farm village."

All around her, kids were still laughing and talking among themselves. It had nothing to do with her. Roseann longed to return to the city and her old, comfortable way of life.

She didn't think she would ever get used to being an outsider.

2

Mr. Wallace was giving the class an assignment to read something about the formation of the Earth when the bell rang, and he made everyone stay until he was finished. Roseann had only three minutes to go all the way downstairs to the gymnasium for her physical education class.

The locker room was wall-to-wall girls, chatting and jostling each other as they pulled on the green gym suits that the teacher had handed them on the way in, along with locks for their baskets. Roseann matched her lock number with the proper basket and dumped her belongings in it, then picked up her gym suit and eyed it critically.

"Vomit green," she said under her breath. "It'll go great with my hair."

Roseann heard a giggle and looked up. Amid the chaos, she hadn't heard the girl with a nearby basket walk up behind her. She must have heard the muttered comment.

"I agree. I think they make us wear these things to add insult to injury." The girl was plain looking but had mischievous eyes.

"Not a phys ed fan, huh?" Roseann commented as she stepped into the one-piece suit.

"Not really. By the way, I'm Allison Tanner. You're new here, right?"

"Right," Roseann told her, tying her sneaker. The girl was direct. Roseann liked that. "I'm Roseann Bellamy."

"I know how you feel." Allison sat down on a bench and began fiddling with her lock. "I was new last year. It was a real pain, especially being from Ohio."

Roseann smiled and looked at Allison with interest. She didn't know that candid people existed in Shelbyville. It makes sense that she's from out of state, Roseann thought wryly.

After dressing, the two girls wound their way through green-clad bodies to the door leading to the gym. Roseann was glad that she didn't have to go out alone. The teacher, Miss Murray, stood outside the door with her whistle around her neck, herding girls toward the bleachers.

Just then, Roseann heard the thump-thump of a basketball at the other end of the gym and glanced in that direction.

There, sinking a basket by reaching close to the rim, was the tallest girl Roseann had ever seen.

The girl had long, dark hair pulled back into a ponytail and was wearing glasses. She had on street clothes—blue shorts and a T-shirt —and black hi-top tennis shoes, the kind the boys wore.

Roseann stared as the girl dribbled and sank one basket after another. No one else seemed to be paying any attention to her as they goofed around on the bleachers with their friends.

Allison grabbed Roseann by the arm, saying, "Come on. Let's go sit near the top. It will drive Murray crazy."

Roseann stood still and kept watching the tall girl, who had stopped to adjust her glasses. They had black frames, the kind no one would be caught dead in except nerdy boys.

Allison stopped and returned to where Roseann was standing.

"Who is that?" Roseann asked. She knew it was rude to stare but couldn't help it.

"Oh, that's Sandy Allen. She's on the varsity basketball team."

"Obviously," said Roseann. "How tall is she, anyway?"

"Over seven feet, I think. She doesn't move very fast. The coach sends her in to get the tip, which she always does. You'll get used to seeing her around."

"There are a LOT of things to get used to around here," Roseann said to herself as the instructor blew her whistle.

The two girls climbed up to one of the high rows in the bleachers as Miss Murray attempted to get the class to be quiet and pay attention. Roseann stole a glance at Sandy Allen, who was depositing her large frame in the second row. She stretched out her long legs and her feet easily reached the gym floor from two rows up. Roseann's mouth dropped open.

The rest of the gym period was spent dividing the students into squads according to alphabetical order—how dorky, Roseann thought —which put her in Sandy's squad. Allison waved and trotted off to the other end of the gym to join the T's-through-Z's.

They did warm-up exercises with Miss Murray pushing everyone to participate. "A point off your grade if you don't," she shouted, eyeing a couple of girls who were just standing around.

When they lined up to shoot baskets, Roseann couldn't take her eyes off Sandy Allen. Her hands were so big that she easily palmed the basketball, and her unerring shots through the hoop looked effortless. Roseann stood next to her, barely coming above Sandy's elbow.

The tall girl wasn't bad-looking, Roseann noticed, but her hair-style wasn't flattering and her glasses were too masculine. Sandy's arms and legs were thin, but with her large bones Roseann guessed that she probably weighed over 300 pounds.

Roseann watched as Sandy sank a basket from about 15 feet away, then went to sit on the bleachers to rest. She pulled a handkerchief out of her pocket and wiped the sweat from her face.

Impulsively, Roseann walked over to her. "Nice shot," she commented.

The tall girl smiled self-consciously. "Thanks," she said in a deep, masculine voice. She lowered her eyes as if she were embarrassed.

"You're good," Roseann rambled on. "I guess it helps to be tall."

"That's about all it's good for," Sandy replied, looking squarely at the red-haired girl. Sitting down, Sandy was the same height as Rose-ann was standing up.

"Oh," Roseann said, taken aback. "I'm sorry. I didn't mean . . ."

Sandy offered a half-smile and held a large hand up in the air.

"That's OK," she said. "Don't mind me, I'm just having a bad day."

"Me too," said Roseann. "Well, see you around."

Sandy nodded but didn't say anything. She pushed her glasses up on her nose and looked at the floor.

After class, the girls took their showers, self-consciously covering themselves up with inadequate-sized towels. Not much different from her old school, Roseann noted.

She vied for a position in front of the long locker room mirror and pulled her hair, dampened by the shower, back into a silver ponytail clip. As Roseann was applying her lipstick, she caught a glimpse of Sandy Allen in the mirror.

Sandy, who had been excused five minutes early, already had her skirt and blouse on. She still wore the black hi-tops.

Roseann watched as Sandy put her blue shorts and T-shirt into a basket on the top row, then gathered up her books and ducked under the doorway as she left the locker room.

3

Journalism was her next class, and Roseann was apprehensive. This was where she excelled in her other school, and she wasn't sure what Shelbyville High had to offer, if anything.

She was already late, but she stopped just outside the door and checked inside her notebook to make sure her folder containing clippings of stories she had written was still there. They were her ticket, she hoped, to a place on the school's newspaper staff.

The bell rang just as Roseann appeared in the doorway, and the teacher, a thin, dimpled woman, impatiently waved her into the room. Roseann did a doubletake: She had never seen a teacher wearing jeans and a happy face shirt before. She stifled a laugh and found a seat in the back of the room.

"My name is Mrs. Musgrave," the woman announced as soon as Roseann sat down. "I am the newspaper and yearbook advisor. I expect everyone to come to class on time . . . "—a slight reproachful glance in Roseann's direction—"I give a lot of homework but there is plenty of class time in which to do it, and if you take this class because you think it's a snap course, please get reassigned to a study hall."

Whew! Roseann felt blitzed by this teacher's honesty and a little exhilarated. At least the woman has spirit, she thought.

"Now," Mrs. Musgrave added, "those of you who are interested in being on the newspaper staff, please raise your hands."

Roseann and three others volunteered.

Mrs. Musgrave looked directly at Roseann. "Yes, the red-haired girl in the back, what is your name, please?"

Roseann thought she would die. She hated it when people referred to her carroty hair. Everyone in the room turned to look at her, and she knew her face was turning the same color as her hair.

"Uh, Roseann Bellamy," she said nervously. "I'm a transfer student from North Central High School in Indianapolis."

"And do you have any journalism experience?" the teacher inquired, hoisting herself up on her desk. She was wearing sneakers.

"Well, yes, quite a bit," Roseann managed. "I was a reporter and feature writer on the school paper, and at the end of the term I had been named co-editor for this year." Roseann hoped it didn't sound like bragging, but she felt the need to sell herself.

"I see," said Mrs. Musgrave, peering at the girl over the top of her glasses. "Do you have any samples of your work?"

Roseann pulled out her folder. "Y-yes, I brought some clippings."

"Good," said Mrs. Musgrave. "Leave them on my desk after class."

Roseann dreaded lunch hour. She knew she would probably have to sit by herself in the cafeteria, or with kids she didn't know if there were no empty tables. If she sat by herself, at least she could read a book or finish her letter to Ashley. She didn't know which was worse—being alone, or being with strangers.

She entered the lunchroom and looked around, hoping to spot Allison Tanner. Most of the lunch tables were taken, many of them holding groups of kids who had scooted their chairs over from other tables. A few kids weren't even eating, just talking and fooling around. The pizza and soup line, next to the sandwich and salad line, already was packed with kids.

Roseann did not see Allison and resigned herself to a solitary lunch. She regarded the cold serving line, which had gotten even longer. As she walked to the back of the line, she was startled to hear a couple of voices call out, "Hi Sandy!" She turned in the direction of the greeting, clutching her books. In a corner of the room that previously had been blocked by bodies, not too far from where Roseann had been standing, Sandy Allen sat sideways at a table by herself, one long leg crossed over the other. Two guys who looked like jocks in their letter sweaters and khakis stood nearby.

"How ya doin' tall girl?" one asked, glancing down at the girl's enormous feet in the black hi-tops.

"Just great," she replied in her deep voice, offering a half-smile.

The two guys looked at each other and laughed. "Just great!" they mimicked, making their voices deeper. They shoved each other around and moved away toward another table, still laughing.

Roseann felt a rush of indignation as she watched them walk away. They glanced over their shoulders at Sandy and laughed again. Roseann expected Sandy to be embarrassed by such rudeness, but Sandy was calmly nibbling a sandwich and reading a library book! It hadn't fazed Sandy one bit, it seemed, but Roseann's face was flushed with anger.

I don't believe this, Roseann thought incredulously. She wasn't even bothered by those two jerks!

Roseann stole another glance at Sandy, who still looked unperturbed, then turned back to the lunch line which had moved along without her. As she slid her tray along the stainless steel railing, she thought about joining Sandy for lunch. But by the time Roseann got through the line, she had lost her nerve.

It didn't matter. Sandy Allen's table was already empty.

Roseann's next two classes, Spanish and botany, were boring. No one spoke to her, but a couple of the kids gave her the type of indulgent smiles that are reserved for unfamiliar faces. She sat in the back of the science room and finished her letter to Ashley while pretending to take notes.

Occasionally, her mind drifted back to Sandy Allen and the scene in the cafeteria. Roseann wondered if there were any boys at Shelbyville High who weren't morons. Mostly, though, she wondered about Sandy.

How does she put up with constantly being stared at? Roseann herself was guilty of that. Why does she wear boys' sneakers? Is it because those are all that will fit her? Is her family tall?

To Roseann, Sandy was someone who compelled your attention, distanced from everyone by virtue of her size. Roseann didn't know why, but she felt drawn to the mysterious girl. Maybe it was because she felt distanced from everyone at Shelbyville High too.

Last period was English, Roseann's best subject. She was glad to have it at the end of the day: It gave her something to look forward to.

Clutching her now-dog-eared class schedule, Roseann found the right hallway for her English class. She had managed to find all her classes in the new school without help. Unlike most of her other classrooms, the English room was cheerful and sunny, with bright posters of inspirational sayings on the walls. Roseann recognized quotes from Gibran, Whitman and even Socrates. They made her feel welcome.

The class would be reading *The Catcher in the Rye* and *Light in August*, among other books, the blackboard stated.

At the front of the room was an attractive woman with brown curly hair and wearing glasses—all English teachers wear glasses, Roseann mused—who sized up everyone who walked into the room, nodding and smiling pleasantly when she recognized a student. She had written her name, Mrs. Jeffries, on the blackboard. Roseann got good vibes from the room. English looked like it might be OK.

Roseann walked past the teacher and grabbed a desk by the window in the back, shoving her books on the rack beneath the seat. By now she had a large stack since she hadn't been to her locker all day.

She looked up just in time to see Sandy Allen duck into the doorway, which was several inches below Sandy's head. Mrs. Jeffries looked delighted to have this oversized human being in her class and greeted her by name.

Sandy nodded, expressionless, and started down the aisle next to Roseann's. Without looking around her, Sandy took the desk across the aisle from Roseann, sitting sideways with her legs out in the aisle and the desktop pushing into her midsection. Roseann watched, fascinated. It didn't look like a very comfortable position, but Sandy appeared to be unaffected.

Roseann thought about the cafeteria incident and her sympathizing mood returned. Should she try again to be friendly with this girl? She wasn't open like Roseann's friends in Indianapolis.

Several kids said hello to Sandy and she politely responded. But she seemed detached from those around her. She was definitely a loner, Roseann observed.

Roseann swallowed hard. Suddenly she remembered a past incident, one that might give her some insight into the personality of Sandy Allen.

4

Roseann closed her bedroom door and dumped her schoolbooks on the bed. She had made it into the house and up the stairs without having to answer any probing questions about her first day at Shelbyville High. Her dad was at work, her mom was on the phone, and Scott was nowhere around.

She immediately went to her file cabinet and pulled out the bottom drawer. Kneeling on the floor, she rummaged through several brown folders until she came to the one marked "People." Roseann took out the folder and spread its contents on the floor in front of her. She found what she was looking for: a sheet of paper with an obituary taped to the center. "Tallest Woman Dies," the headline read.

Roseann read the obit, which had run in *The Indianapolis Star* just a few months before. It said:

> Delores Ann Pullard Johnson, believed to be the world's tallest woman, died May 19, 1971, in Houston, Texas. She was 24. Mrs. Johnson, born Aug. 13, 1946, in DeQuincy, La., measured 7 feet 5 inches at the time of her death. For many years she traveled the country, exhibiting herself in circus and state fair sideshows. She married James Johnson, who also worked in the shows. She was billed at a height of 8 feet 2 inches. Services will be private.

A slight chill went through Roseann. When she was nine, she had seen Delores Pullard at the Indiana State Fair. Delores was one of the Midway attractions, exhibited in a large tent with other "Freaks of

Nature," according to the large painted letters on the tent. Delores was billed as "The Amazon Woman," and on the tent was a huge drawing of a reclining African female with several tiny, native males clutching spears and crawling all over her body.

Roseann was at the fair with her parents and two of her cousins, a couple of rowdy boys close to her own age. The boys begged to go into the tent, and their enthusiasm had piqued Roseann's interest. Her parents refused to go but bought tickets for the children.

It was a typical, hot August day, and the tent was sweltering inside, Roseann remembered, smelling like a mixture of sweat and cow dung. She had difficulty breathing, with everyone squashed together in a line that snaked along a rope railing.

The first exhibit they came to was a midget billed as Mighty Mite, who stood on a platform telling jokes and bantering with the crowd. A sign said that he was "three feet tall with the strength of a man twice his height." But he wasn't performing any feats of strength that day. He chatted and did a little dance and insulted a couple of large men in the audience, which made everyone laugh, including Roseann. There was a jar for donations near the rope, and it was full of tip money.

Anxious to see what they came in for, the two boys pulled Roseann along, past a couple of other exhibits, toward a line moving slowly past the area with an "Amazon Woman" sign suspended above. Roseann figured it was some kind of trickery, that no one could be as big as the woman whose figure was painted on the tent. They couldn't see past what was mostly an adult crowd, so they inched their way along, craning their necks ahead.

Finally, their turn came. Roseann found herself standing in front of—not an exotic Amazon woman—but a large black woman in a wheelchair. She wore a baggy print dress and no shoes. Sweating profusely, the woman used a handheld fan to swat flies away from her face. She watched a small, black-and-white TV perched near her on a box. A large Coke sat on another box. A few feet away, a portable fan whirred with minimal effect.

In front of her was a small sign that said she was "Delores Pullard, Southern Negress" and that she was over eight feet tall.

One of Roseann's cousins said "Wow!" while the other one demanded to see Delores's hand. The woman held her hand out, palm up, and the boys took turns putting their small palms up against hers. Their entire hands with spread fingers barely covered her palm.

The boys pelted Delores with questions: How tall are you? How much do you eat? How much do you weigh? The woman answered each question in a deep-voiced monotone without taking her eyes off the TV.

"Look at her feet!" one of the boys said, as if the woman wasn't there.

"Will you stand up?" asked the other boy. "We want to see how tall you are."

Delores shook her head no and pointed to the wheelchair, which had been made oversized to hold her large frame.

Roseann felt sick. This woman exhibited herself to make a living because she was big. She wasn't like Mighty Mite, who seemed to be having a good time at it. Instead, she looked tired and sad. Roseann was embarrassed about her cousins' loud insensitivity, and embarrassed for Delores, who answered all of their questions flatly, as if she had heard them dozens of times. She probably had.

Roseann's heart was pounding. The heat and smell in the tent made her dizzy. She wanted to say something nice to the woman, but all she could do was stare. The line moved along until Roseann was right in front of Delores. She spotted the tip jar, dug into her pocket and pulled out all the change she had, 57 cents. She threw it into the jar and mumbled, "It was nice meeting you." She couldn't even look at Delores. Then she fled from the tent as fast as she could.

Her cousins came out a few minutes later, exclaiming excitedly to her parents about what they had just seen. Roseann was silent for the rest of the day and didn't enjoy the fair. All she could think about was Delores Pullard, sweating and swatting flies in the tent.

The experience had a great impact on Roseann: For months afterward she thought about the tall, sad young woman and wondered if she still had to work in sideshow tents. Had Delores ever been happy or had any friends? She also wondered how Delores got so tall.

A few years later, she found Delores's obituary in *The Star*. The news of her death depressed Roseann for days. She cut out the obit and added it to her collection of articles on interesting people, which she kept in her files. As an avid reader and writer, Roseann saved anything interesting in file folders, tucked away for future reference.

Curiously, Roseann mourned Delores Pullard's death as if she were a friend. She wondered who this Johnson person was that the tall woman apparently had married. Maybe he was one of those hotshot promoters who makes money off of exhibiting people, she thought angrily.

Looking at the obituary, the entire Delores/State Fair scene came back to Roseann, a scene that blurred into that of Sandy Allen, sitting in the high school cafeteria in her black hi-tops, with two teenage boys making fun of her. Roseann's mind replayed all three of her encounters that day with Sandy. She had the same voice as Delores, the same emotionless responses to people reacting to her, the same tired, sad look of resignation.

I want to do something, Roseann thought with determination.

She gathered up the papers she had spread out and assembled them back into her "People" folder, putting Delores Pullard Johnson's obit on top. She placed the folder back into her file cabinet and took out a notebook to make a list.

She knew exactly what she had to do.

5

Sandy Allen stepped off the school bus a block from her house. She hoped that nothing had happened to Joey that day.

The seven-foot-three-inch girl always hated the first day of school: There were too many kids who had never seen her before, so the comments and staring and teasing were in high gear. The boys were the worst. They considered her their own personal target, mimicking her voice and following her down the hall, copying her walk. The school counselor told her it was because of their own lack of self-confidence, that making fun of someone else gave them a feeling of superiority. It didn't help. Sandy wished they'd all drop dead.

A couple of neighbor kids called out to her as she walked by and she waved to them. They were used to her size and their small offerings of attention made her feel good. She loved little kids, especially her little brother, Joey, who had just turned four.

Sandy quickened her pace as she thought of him. She needed to get home right away to see if he was all right.

Her depression over the school day increased as she approached her house, a weatherbeaten, yellowish clapboard dwelling on Hamilton Street. It was her grandmother's house and four people lived in its four rooms, not counting the bathroom that had been added on several years ago. And I'm big enough for two, Sandy mused.

It wasn't much more than a shack. The rest of the houses on the block, although not much bigger, had been kept up better. But Sandy's family couldn't afford that, and she vowed that when she got a job, she'd help her granny fix it up. Meanwhile, people stared at Sandy's house as often as they stared at her.

Sandy dug into her purse and pulled out an apple, a daily treat for Joey. She always saved him an apple from her lunch. Shifting her schoolbooks to her left arm, she went up the steps to the house and opened the screen door with her right hand, letting it slam loudly behind her. Might as well let the witch know I'm home, she thought darkly.

Sandy was relieved to find things in order. Joey was sitting on the oversized bed that Sandy shared with her grandmother in the second room, the one between the living room and kitchen. He was watching TV but jumped down and ran to Sandy when she ducked through the doorway into the room.

"Apple, Sissy?" he asked, wide-eyed. Sandy smiled and handed it to him: He hadn't forgotten the treat from last year.

She lifted him back up on the bed and checked him for bruises while he returned to watching the TV show, happily munching on his apple. Their Aunt Violet poked her head around the corner and frowned at them.

"Oh, it's you," she snarled at Sandy. "Good. You can entertain him for a while." She disappeared into her bedroom off the back of the kitchen.

Sandy made a face toward her aunt's retreating back, restraining herself from offering a snide remark.

Sandy had been raised by her grandmother, Dora, and called her Granny or Mom. Her mother, Vera, who had shown up three years ago when Joey was a baby, had gone off to Florida with her latest boyfriend and never came back. She gave custody of Joey to one of her sisters, a childless widow who eventually came to live with Sandy and Dora, bringing Joey with her.

A heavy-set, disagreeable woman who often drank too much, Aunt Violet ("More like 'Violence,'" Sandy was fond of saying to anyone who would listen) received welfare checks for herself and the children, and

Dora was grateful for the extra money coming in, although much of it went to Violet's drinking habit. On the first of the month, the welfare checks arrived. By the second of the month, Vi had usually drunk it all or spent it on lottery tickets.

Dora cleaned houses several days a week to supplement her small Social Security check. Vi did most of the family's cooking and cleaning, and Dora was grateful for the help.

Sandy dreaded telling her aunt that she would need money for this year's schoolbooks, but she knew she had to do it. She sighed heavily and went to the doorway of her bedroom.

"Vi!" she shouted in her booming voice. "I need to talk to you."

"What do you want?" Violet appeared in the doorway with a scowl on her face. Joey leaped from the bed and tore into the bathroom, slamming the door. Sometimes Violet took her anger out on him.

"I need money for school," Sandy told her. It was a simple request, but she knew Vi would make it into a big deal.

"You always want something," Vi said with a snort.

"No, I don't," Sandy retorted. "But if you can't give it to me, I'll ask Granny for it."

"Go ahead," she snapped. "You think I'm made of money? You and Joey, you always want something."

Sandy bristled. "Believe me, if I had a choice, I wouldn't ask you for a dime!"

Violet narrowed her eyes and walked toward Sandy, then pushed her way past her niece. Go ahead, Sandy thought, you wouldn't dare lay a hand on me.

Sandy sighed as Violet busied herself in the living room, muttering about a lampshade she didn't like. Sandy shook her head at her aunt's goofy behavior, then walked across the bedroom and knocked on the door of the adjoining bathroom. "It's OK now," she said.

After several minutes, Joey finally came out. His half-eaten apple lay on the linoleum. Sandy picked it up and looked over her shoulder to make sure Vi wasn't watching. The floor was filthy, so she went into the bathroom and threw the apple in the trash.

Sandy forgot all about her rotten day at school.

6

"Will Dad be home for dinner?" Roseann asked, getting the dishes out of the cupboard.

"I don't think so, honey," her mother told her. "He got tied up in some meeting with the hospital's Board of Directors."

"Sounds boring," Roseann murmured, setting three dishes around the kitchen table. They only ate in the dining room when her father was home.

Roseann's nine-year-old brother, Scott, appeared in the doorway. "Can I eat in front of the TV?" he wanted to know.

"Not tonight," their mother answered. "I want to hear about your first day at school."

"Jeez," said Scott, slumping into a chair. Suddenly, he brightened. "I had a GREAT day at school! NOW can I eat in front of the TV? Please?"

Barbara Bellamy smiled at her son. They had the same dark good looks, with brown eyes and olive skin. Scott's hair was thick and wavy, the kind that Roseann would kill for. But she was stuck with carroty hair like her father's, and wore it in the latest style, long and straight. She also had his grayish eyes, which she considered weird.

Roseann thought her mother was beautiful, but in a way that was beyond attractiveness. She was patient and loving—especially with Scott, who was high strung—and had a fun personality. She was the most perfect person that Roseann knew.

Well, almost. Roseann also thought her mother was too lenient where Scott was concerned. Because of his hyperactivity, he lacked concentration in school and often was disruptive at home. It taxed the patience of Roseann and her father, and Barbara Bellamy often gave in to Scott to keep peace. It caused contention in the home from time to time. Still, it was no surprise when her mother told him to go ahead and serve himself and eat in the living room.

Roseann sighed and handed Scott a plate, which he grabbed without looking at her.

"You're WELCOME," she told him sarcastically.

Scott stuck out his tongue at her, then loaded his plate with tuna noodle casserole. They ate casseroles a lot these days: They were easy for her father to warm up when he had to work late.

"What a rude brat," Roseann muttered as he rushed past her and out of the kitchen.

"Now honey, you should have more patience with him. He's in a new environment and he needs to be able to count on routine things to make him feel secure," her mother said. "TV isn't a big deal."

(Her dad, she thought, would have told her, "Check your attitude at the door," his current favorite phrase.)

"Besides, I'd like to hear about your day," her mother emphasized.

As much as Roseann enjoyed having a few moments to herself with her mom, she wasn't all that eager to share Shelbyville High with her. If she told her what she really thought about the school, it would just disappoint her. If she lied, her mother would see right through it; she was uncanny that way.

She opted for reality.

"Well," she said, "it was just like I thought. The building is time-warped to World War II and the kids are, well, different from the ones in Indianapolis. My teachers are OK. The history teacher is kinda creepy and definitely isn't Mr. Kotter, but my journalism teacher is fun. That's about it."

Barbara Bellamy frowned. Here comes the guilt trip, Roseann thought, bracing herself.

Instead, her mother reached over and patted her on the arm.

"I know it's hard because it's so different" Her tone was sympathetic. "But you'll get used to it. There have to be some nice kids you can be friends with. And a building is just a building. It's what you learn there that counts. If you were being a superstar on the newspaper at your other school, where there was so much competition, think what you can accomplish here! By Christmas, you'll have things just as well in hand here as you did in Indianapolis."

Roseann gave her a wan smile. "I don't think so," she said, "but thanks for the vote of confidence."

"Any time," said her mom, putting a serving of tuna cooked with crushed potato chips and peas on Roseann's plate.

Her mother chatted on about meeting Scott's teacher that day and what his school was like. Sounds from *The Partridge Family* drifted in from the living room, and every now and then Scott would burst into laughter.

Roseann listened with one ear and made what she hoped were proper responses to her mother's rundown of the day. She was more occupied with thoughts of Sandy Allen—and Delores Pullard. She knew that her mother would be interested in her encounter with Sandy. But she wasn't quite ready to share Sandy with her family yet. She needed more time to think about her plan to get to know her tall classmate.

7

Roseann spent the rest of the week observing Sandy Allen. It was fairly easy, having two classes with her as well as lunch hour. She wondered if the boys teasing Sandy in the cafeteria was an isolated incident, or if it was a common occurrence. It was. Most of the teasing came from boys, Roseann noted, but a group of stuck-up girls in her gym class had giggled behind her back in the locker room.

There were nice people too: Every day people spoke to Sandy, but not many extended themselves beyond polite greetings. Sandy didn't appear to have many friends, although Roseann saw her occasionally walk down the hall with a blond girl named Carole, who was in Roseann's botany class. Sandy always walked with her head bent, as if she were trying to make herself look smaller.

Gym class gave Roseann the best opportunity to watch Sandy up close, especially since they were in the same squads and on many of the same teams. She tried to observe her without being obvious, not wanting to seem like another gawker.

At lunch Sandy often paid for her meal with a green piece of paper. Every day Roseann saw Sandy get an apple, but she never ate it, just put it in her purse. After a quick meal, the tall girl mysteriously disappeared for the rest of the period.

In English class, Sandy always had her homework done but never volunteered in class. If Mrs. Jeffries called on her, she always knew the answer. She obviously was intelligent, Roseann noted, she just didn't take risks.

Of course, neither did Roseann, not in this school. It was real easy to close yourself off from everyone and tend to your own business. Roseann ached for North Central High, where she was with kids she had known since grade school, and her classes were progressive. At Shelbyville High, she felt that she had taken ten steps backwards.

But Roseann knew she was fairly smart and was a diligent—if not gifted—writer. Given a chance, she could excel, she thought. She looked at Sandy and wondered what her options were. Sandy couldn't even sit comfortably at a normal desk.

Neither, she imagined, could Delores.

By the time a couple of weeks had passed, Roseann had become acquainted with Julie Jackson, a bright and witty girl in her journalism class who also wrote and edited for the school paper. Julie was outgoing and friendly to everyone and was always joking around. But she took her writing seriously, and Roseann was intrigued by Julie's ability to balance fun and work. Roseann got so tied up in her own projects that she often forgot to have a good time.

One day, Mrs. Musgrave called Roseann up to her desk.

"Your work is very impressive," she said, handing Roseann the folder with her clippings from the year before. "We certainly could use you on the *Courier* staff. How do you feel about feature writing? You could do other things, too, but you seem to have a way of going beyond the ordinary to capture the subjects in your feature interviews."

Roseann beamed. "I'd love to," she told the teacher. "I think that's what I do best."

Mrs. Musgrave smiled, showing those dimples that were big enough to plant flowers in. "Good. Starting next week, every Tuesday and Thursday you'll report to the newspaper office during class. On those days, the rest of the class will do assignments while you work on a story for the next issue. Julie Jackson and Randy Kozlowski are co-editors, and they can help you if I'm not available."

Roseann tucked her folder into her notebook. "Thank you," she said. "Thank you so much."

Now I can put my idea to work, she thought, smiling knowingly to herself.

Julie caught up with Roseann after their third period journalism class as she walked toward the cafeteria. After congratulating her on her appointment to the newspaper staff, Julie asked Roseann about her lunch plans.

"Don't have any," Roseann shrugged. "I don't know many people yet."

"Problem solved!" Julie announced. "We need someone to bus our table."

Roseann looked at her curiously.

"It was a joke," explained the dark-hair girl, pretending to be exasperated.

Roseann looked at her and laughed—the first time she had laughed in an entire month. And the first time she had someone to eat lunch with at Shelbyville High.

That day, Roseann watched as Sandy Allen went through the hot food line and paid for her meal with the green piece of paper. She leaned over to Julie and asked what it was, nodding toward the cashier where Sandy was standing head and shoulders above everyone else.

"It's a lunch voucher," Julie told her.

"What's that?" Roseann asked. The other two girls at their table snickered.

"It's a school district program that provides free lunches for kids who can't afford it," Julie explained.

"Kind of like welfare?"

"Yeah, kind of."

"Oh." Roseann had heard about welfare programs, but thought it was for poor people who lived in the inner city, like in Indianapolis. No one at her old township school was on welfare—at least, none that she knew of. They were mostly middle and upper-middle-class families. Several were very well off.

"Sandy Allen's family is on welfare," Julie said with a sympathetic smile. She didn't want Roseann to be embarrassed. "A lot of people around here are. It's no big wazoo."

Roseann nodded. She turned to watch Sandy carry her tray to the table where she usually sat by herself. Several other heads turned to watch the giant girl, too. Julie was talking with her friends at their table, leaving Roseann alone with her thoughts.

How many secrets does Sandy Allen have, she pondered.

She had a feeling there were a lot.

8

Sandy Allen closed the bathroom door and pulled the string attached to the ceiling light. The bare bulb brightened the room, which had no windows, and Sandy ducked to avoid hitting her head on the fixture.

With her stomach heaving, she sat on the edge of the bathtub and opened the lid of the toilet in case she threw up. She picked up a roll of toilet paper from the floor and tore off several sections, making sure she didn't use too much. Vi, she thought sarcastically, wouldn't want her to waste it. Sandy clutched her stomach with one hand and wiped the sweat from her brow with the other.

I just can't go to school today, she thought miserably.

Sandy thought that maybe this year would be different; that circumstances at home would improve and the teasing about her size would die down. Instead, both had gotten worse. Anxiety plagued her constantly, and along with the anxiety came the morning heaves, which always sent her to the bathroom, sometimes for as long as half an hour. She started setting the alarm clock earlier in case she had to take care of her sickness before leaving for school.

Sandy sat on the edge of the tub for several minutes, and eventually the nausea subsided. She was glad she didn't throw up: It hurt too much. Her forehead was still dripping with sweat. Sandy looked behind her at all of the clothes piled up in the bathtub, which was not hooked up to the plumbing. The tub had become a big laundry hamper, full of dirty clothes as well as clothes her family didn't wear anymore. Washing clothes meant a trip to the Laundromat for her and her granny.

She pulled an old pair of shorts out of the pile and held it to her head, soaking up the sweat. The shorts didn't fit her anymore: All of her clothes were getting shorter and tighter, she noticed. Her hands, nearly three times the size of a normal-sized person's hands, also seemed bigger to her, and her feet were getting more and more cramped from stuffing them into size 16EEE men's shoes—the only kind that fit her.

Sandy held out her right hand, palm up, then turned it over. Someone once told her that her fingers looked like hot dogs, and it had badly hurt her feelings. Then her family had hot dogs for dinner one night and she discovered that her fingers were even larger than the wieners they were eating. She couldn't finish her dinner.

She stared at her hand for a long time. She had thought that by the time she was 16, she wouldn't get any bigger, but her body wasn't listening. I must still be growing, she thought with alarm. Pretty soon I won't even fit in this stupid, rundown little house!

She stood up and leaned way over to look in the bathroom mirror. Even her face was changing, she observed, as she ran her hand over her forehead just above her eyes. Her protruding forehead seemed to be more pronounced than a few months ago, her temples sunken in at the sides. Sandy hated her broad nose and thought her lips were too full. Looking inside her mouth, she noticed that her teeth were starting to get spaces between them. Her bones seemed to be outgrowing her features.

God, I'm ugly, Sandy thought, regarding her image through the smudged glass. Ugly and big, and getting uglier and bigger by the minute. I don't know if I can go through another day feeling like the freak of Shelbyville.

She covered her face with her hands and stood there for a minute, pulling herself together. I can't do this, she thought as her mind wrestled with her feelings. She ended up saying a prayer, asking God to make things better. Her religious upbringing was about all she had left to depend on, and even that was getting shaky.

Sandy wiped her face and brushed her thick, dark hair, which hung past her shoulders. She knew that going to school was important that day: She had a chance to join the Sunshine Society, a social service organization, and her English teacher, Mrs. Jeffries, was the group's advisor. The teacher had been encouraging Sandy to participate in the group's humanitarian projects. She couldn't let Mrs. Jeffries down. Most of all, she couldn't let herself down.

She'd just have to figure out a way to not worry so much about Joey.

9

Roseann burst into the *Courier* office three minutes early. She was pleased to find Julie Jackson already there, cleaning out files from the previous year.

"Has anyone ever done a story on Sandy Allen?" Roseann inquired, dumping her books on a cluttered desk. The office was small and didn't look very organized. To Roseann, it seemed to be an afterthought, tucked into a tiny space at the top of the stairway of the English wing.

"What?" Julie looked up, her short, dark hair falling in her eyes.

"Sandy Allen," Roseann repeated. "Has the *Courier* ever done a feature on her?"

Julie frowned, looking thoughtful. "No, I don't think so. What did you have in mind?" She unwrapped a piece of Bazooka bubble gum and stuck it in her mouth.

Roseann shoved over some file folders and hoisted herself up on one of the two desks in the room. Julie was on the floor, sitting cross-legged in front of the bottom drawer of a file cabinet that looked like a Civil War relic.

"Well," she began, "there's the obvious angle of her being so tall, probably the tallest person—let alone a girl—to play for the Golden Bears."

Julie nodded and waited for Roseann to continue.

"Then there's the personal angle," Roseann ventured. "Most kids seem to either tease her or ignore her. Maybe if they learned more about her, and the problems someone her size faces, she would be less

. . . you know . . . misunderstood."

Julie took the folder she had been looking at and stuck it back into the file cabinet. Then she picked up a pile of loose papers scattered on the floor and shoved them into a wastebasket. "It's OK with me. You'll have to run it by Musgrave," she said without much enthusiasm.

Roseann sensed her editor's hesitation. "But?" she asked, raising her eyebrows so that they disappeared under her bangs.

Julie stood up and faced Roseann, chewing vigorously on the gum. "Could be a problem," she said.

Roseann looked at her questioningly.

"Sandy's not very . . . you know . . . social. She doesn't interact with other kids very well. She's very private. You might have a rough time getting her to agree to an interview."

"I think I can handle it," Roseann told her confidently.

"Then go for it, Bellamy, as long as the boss agrees."

Roseann smiled at the way Julie called people by their last names, like they sometimes did in old hotshot reporter movies about newspapers. Julie was personable but no-nonsense, so she got away with it.

"Thanks!" Roseann told her, jumping off the desk and surveying the messy room. "Now, what can I help you with?"

10

Roseann finished out the period helping Julie sort through back issues of the *Courier* and clean out file cabinets. As soon as that hour's journalism class was over, Roseann popped in to run her story idea past Mrs. Musgrave. With her approval, Roseann headed for the cafeteria alone, since Julie had brought her lunch that day so she could continue working in the newspaper office.

Maybe I'll talk to Sandy about the story today, Roseann thought with anticipation.

Sandy Allen was halfway through the hot lunch line when Roseann got there. She was surprised to see Sandy eating a sloppy Joe: Sandy had sat out the entire gym period that day with a stomachache. Boy, I hope she feels like talking to me, Roseann thought as she joined the end of the sandwich line.

She watched as Sandy took long strides to her usual table and carefully lowered herself into the too-small cafeteria chair. Several kids turned to stare. Roseann paid for her lunch, then walked purposefully toward where Sandy was sitting. She didn't care if anyone was watching her.

"Hi," she said, putting her tray down opposite Sandy's. "OK if I sit here?"

Sandy looked up, startled. "Sure," she said uncertainly. "You're in my gym class."

"English, too," Roseann replied as she sat down. "I'm Roseann Bellamy. I sit across from you."

"Oh." Sandy looked embarrassed but Roseann ignored it.

"Anyway," Roseann went on, "it's nice to find a familiar face in here. I don't know very many people in this school yet."

Sandy looked up from her sandwich, which had all but disappeared into her huge hand. It was just like Delores's hand, Roseann noted uncomfortably.

Sandy didn't respond, and Roseann sensed that small talk wasn't going to be forthcoming. Nearby, a table full of boys watched them with interest.

"Hey! Bigfoot!" one of them yelled, pointing to Sandy's feet in the black hi-tops. The others at his table laughed.

Roseann turned and glared at them, feeling her neck getting hot. Sandy looked down at her lunch tray. Then, as if nothing had happened, she took a bite of her sandwich.

Roseann opened her mouth to say something, then closed it again.

"Better get used to it if you're going to eat lunch with me." Sandy's deep voice broke into her thoughts, which were bordering on homicide. Roseann looked at Sandy incredulously.

"Are YOU used to it?" she blurted out.

Sandy's reply was simple. "I've had it nearly all my life. Most of the time I can tune it out,"

Roseann slowly unwrapped her ham and cheese sandwich. The image of Delores tuning out comments of onlookers in the sideshow tent flashed through her mind. Roseann had run away then: Too young and too helpless to do anything. I won't run away this time, she determined.

Changing the subject seemed to be a safe thing to do.

"Actually, there's something I wanted to talk to you about," Roseann said, trying hard not to look at the table full of jerks.

"There is?" Sandy looked at her curiously, pushing her black-rimmed glasses up on her nose with a giant finger. She wasn't used to people seeking her out for anything, let alone joining her for lunch.

"Yes," Roseann said carefully, popping open a carton of milk. "I just got on the newspaper staff—you know, the *Courier*—and I'd like to do a story on you." She paused to let this information sink in. Sandy said nothing. "You're obviously a terrific basketball player," Roseann added.

"You want to talk about basketball?" Sandy asked.

"Well, not just that." Roseann took a deep breath, choosing her words carefully.

"There must be some really unique, um, problems connected with being so tall. And some advantages, too," she added quickly. "Maybe if people understood what it's like to be your size, they wouldn't hassle you so much."

Roseann held her breath while Sandy absorbed all of this. She had stopped eating and was looking down, a habit Roseann noticed from the first day she saw her. Roseann stole a glance toward the boys at the next table. Now they were staring at HER. She turned away quickly.

Suddenly, Sandy looked up at her.

"I hope you don't want to do this because you feel sorry for me," she said evenly.

Roseann felt disarmed. She hadn't expected that reaction!

"No, of course not," she said in what she hoped wasn't too defensive a tone. Maybe Julie was right: Sandy might be too shy to be interviewed. She certainly was visible enough without having a newspaper story written about her!

Roseann watched as Sandy pushed her milk carton around on her tray, not making eye contact.

"Look," Roseann said earnestly," "I have an idea. You can have first look at whatever I write about you. If you don't like it, it's history. OK?"

Sandy was silent for what seemed like an eternity.

"I work as a library assistant first period," she said finally. "Is that a good time to do this?"

Roseann breathed a sigh of relief. "I don't know, I'll have to see if I can get out of class." No history! What a break! "When I find out something, I'll let you know."

"OK," said Sandy. "I really have to go," she said suddenly.

Roseann watched as Sandy stood up and towered over her, gathering up her lunch tray. The boys at the next table hooted.

"Hey, Bigfoot's leaving!" one of them shouted.

Sandy looked down at Roseann. "If you change your mind, it won't bother me," she said in her mannish voice.

Roseann glared at the boys, then looked up at Sandy and smiled. "I won't," she promised.

11

"Scott! Get your butt in here!"

Roseann was furious. She had come home from school in a good mood: Her interview with Sandy Allen had been approved. But when she got to her bedroom, several things on her desk were out of order. Her jar of pens and pencils was tipped over, a box of staples had spilled and two drawers were pulled halfway out. She knew her little brother was the culprit—it wasn't the first time Scott had "borrowed" something from her and left a mess. Roseann hated messes. Everything she owned was in its proper place.

Why do I have a brother who is both sneaky and a slob? she thought irritably.

Scott appeared in the doorway, looking guilty.

"What did you take?" Roseann demanded. "And why were you in my room? You know that makes me mad."

"This is my house, too," he said defensively. "I can go anywhere I want."

"No, you can't. This is my room, and I'll put a lock on the door if I have to. I don't go in your scummy room. Now, what did you take?"

"I needed to borrow your tape recorder. " He stuck out his chin defiantly.

"Are you brain dead?" Roseann shouted. "I never let anyone borrow my tape recorder, let alone a little brat like you! Now bring it back!"

"Mom said you have a bad temper because of your red hair," Scott announced, sticking out his tongue. He turned and stomped down the hall toward his bedroom.

"I have a bad temper because I have a snotty little brother like you!" she called after him.

Still angry, Roseann started straightening up her room. Scott had pulled out all her file cabinet drawers and two in her desk. She usually kept important things, like her journal and her good pens, hidden from him, but since the move to this house she hadn't bothered to find new hiding places. Guess I'd better make that a priority, she grumbled to herself.

Scott made a lot of noise coming down the hall, but stopped when he got to her doorway.

"Is it OK if I come into your stupid room?" he asked with mock politeness. He had the small, portable tape recorder in his hand.

"No, it isn't," said Roseann, walking toward him with her hand out. "Now give it back and don't ever take it again!"

Scott narrowed his eyes as she approached him, then glanced beyond her toward the bed, which wasn't too far from the door. "Here's your precious tape recorder," he sneered. Roseann watched in disbelief as Scott raised his hand to throw it. She grabbed for it but Scott was too quick for her and flung it past her toward the bed. She stood frozen as it landed on the edge of the bed, then slid off onto the floor with a crash. The lid popped open when it landed.

Scott's eyes widened, then he raced off down the hall and down the stairway to the kitchen.

Roseann was so stunned that she couldn't even yell at him. She picked up the tape recorder, which had been a birthday present a couple of years ago. She pushed the lid down but it popped back up again. The little plastic catch had broken off. "Stupid little jerk!" she muttered.

She knew that she was too old to tattle on him to her parents, who would just defend him anyway, especially her mother. She'd remind Roseann that Scott's hyperactivity caused him to do a lot of spontaneous acts that he was always sorry about later. Sorry won't fix my tape recorder, she thought bitterly.

Roseann went over to her desk and found a roll of masking tape. She tore off a piece and taped the lid down. Then she rewound the audio tape that was still inside it and played it. The recorder still worked.

I'll let him get by with this one, she thought. But next time he might not be so lucky.

12

Sandy Allen took the late bus home after her Sunshine Society meeting, which had gone well. Her feeling of accomplishment was short-lived, though: Her house was in chaos when she got home from school. Violet was on one of her rampages and Sandy could hear her shouting all the way from the bus stop. She rushed down the street and found Joey cowering in the side yard, crying. He wasn't wearing a shirt and there were scratch marks on his arm.

Sandy threw her books on the ground and scooped up her little brother, hugging him close. Joey clung to her and sobbed while Sandy listened to their aunt scream obscenities in the house. Should she go in and see what was going on and make sure that Dora was all right? It was rare that Violet physically abused them, but Granny and Joey became scared when she shouted and cursed.

A couple of neighbors across the street came out on their front porch and stared toward Sandy's house. They shook their heads and went back inside as Sandy turned her back on them, still holding the crying child.

"Can you tell me what happened, honey?" Sandy asked her brother. She patted his back and talked to him soothingly, trying to calm him down. She heard a crash and stole an anxious glance toward the house.

"My b-bike, Sissy. S-she has my b-bike," Joey told her between sobs.

Adrenalin, mixed with fear and anger, raced through Sandy's body. She put Joey down on the grass. "Stay here in the yard!" she

39

commanded. "Just stay here and don't move. I'll be right back."

Sandy rushed around the corner of the house and flung open the front door. She came face-to-face with Violet, who stood in the living room holding an axe. In front of her was Joey's blue tricycle which their grandmother had bought him for his birthday.

She quickly looked around—the house was in more disarray than usual—then back at Violet, who was standing there in her nightgown, drunk and angry, clutching the axe handle with both hands.

"You're not going to stop me this time!" Vi shouted as she raised the axe into the air. Dora stood behind her, covering her face with her hands.

"Put that down, you fatass dingbat!" Sandy yelled, taking a step forward. She started to grab for the axe but it was too late. Vi brought it crashing down onto the tricycle, making a huge dent in the seat. Her next swing chopped off a wheel. Sandy watch helplessly as Vi swung a third time and just barely grazed the handlebars, splitting the rubber grip. Vi stumbled unsteadily under the weight of the axe and her drunkenness, and Sandy lunged forward and wrestled the tool away from the screaming woman.

"No! Nooooo!" Joey stood outside the screen door, crying and looking at his bike. Sandy whirled around with the axe in her hand. "Go back in the yard!" she told him.

Consumed with anger, Sandy raised the axe and took a step toward her aunt, who was shouting, "Serves him right! Serves the little brat right!"

"I'll serve you right," Sandy growled as she took another step toward Violet.

Dora rushed up behind Vi and dragged her toward the kitchen. Vi's screaming subsided into muttering. "Little brat," she was saying over and over. "That'll teach him to spill Kool-Aid on the floor."

Sandy lowered the axe and glared furiously at her aunt.

"You did this because of some stupid Kool-Aid?" Sandy shouted. "He's only four years old! You should be locked up in some nut house!"

Sandy looked down at the battered bike and felt defeated. She knew that her aunt was really crazy, and that they still had a long evening ahead of them. Then she turned and went back outside to comfort Joey, who was still crying. She'd somehow try to figure out how to fix the bike.

One of these days, she thought, I won't be able to stop myself. It would be a pleasure to give that tub of lard a taste of her own medicine.

The next morning, Sandy got out of bed carefully so she wouldn't wake up her grandmother and brother. Joey had slept with them last night, too scared to sleep in the room he shared with Violet. Fortunately, their aunt hadn't stuck around after the bike-bashing. She had gotten dressed and headed downtown— probably to the taverns, Sandy thought with disgust—and didn't come home until around 3 a.m. Sandy heard her come in: She had learned to be a light sleeper where Violet was concerned. With a little brother and an elderly woman to look after, she could never be too careful.

As soon as Sandy got up, her stomach lurched. She made it into the bathroom just in time to throw up. Sandy sat on the floor for a long time, clutching the toilet bowl and waiting for the nausea to pass. I just can't go to school today, she thought. It was getting harder and harder to leave the house in the mornings.

Sandy had almost forgotten what she had to do that day: Roseann, the girl from the newspaper staff, wanted to interview her. Of all days to have to talk to someone! But then, there's never a good day. Why can't everyone just leave me alone? she thought miserably.

After sitting on the floor for a while, Sandy started to feel better. She stood up and wiped the sweat off her face, then brushed her teeth and hair. Opening the bathroom door, she walked quietly through the bedroom—which was really the house's dining room—where Joey and her grandmother were still sleeping. She entered the kitchen and leaned down through the doorway to look into Violet's room. Her aunt was passed out on the bed, still in her street clothes, and was snoring

41

loudly. The old bag will probably sleep all day, Sandy noted, turning away quickly so she didn't have to look at the woman.

Sandy decided to go to school. At noon, when she made her daily phone call to Joey, she would figure out if she needed to come home. It wouldn't be the first time she played sick and had the school nurse bring her home.

Sandy went over to the stove and turned on the tea kettle, then ran some cold water into a large pan for a sponge bath. As soon as the hot water was ready, she poured it into the pan and set it on the kitchen table. When her great-grandfather had built the bathroom onto the house a few years ago, he had put in a hot water heater, but the connection to the tub was no longer working, so they couldn't take baths or showers. And they couldn't afford to get it fixed right now. They always did without so much, Sandy thought bitterly. Violet blew the welfare money on whatever she pleased and didn't seem to care that Dora worked almost every day while she stayed home and watched soap operas on TV. It was an injustice that angered Sandy daily.

But she couldn't think about that now. As she took her bath, Sandy thought about what kind of questions Roseann was likely to ask her. She liked the little red-haired girl: She seemed to be friendly enough and was not put off by Sandy's size. But what could Sandy tell her? That aside from basketball, being over seven feet tall was a horrible, freaky thing that she didn't wish on anybody? That every day she wanted to shrink down to normal size? That the teasing and gawking hurt her so badly that it put a huge, twisted knot in her stomach and she had to pretend that it wasn't there? She couldn't tell Roseann all that any more than she could announce that she'd like to toss her aunt into the Big Blue River.

There were so many things to hide and no place to hide them.

She'd just have to do the best she could, Sandy decided, and steer away from any questions about her family. She'd wear her new green dress that her granny had made for her and the mail-order shoes she had just gotten out of a men's catalog. And she'd talk about basketball.

13

Early the next morning Roseann pulled the chair out from her desk and placed it near her bed. She measured the chair from seat to floor: Only 18 inches, she discovered. She hurried downstairs into the living room, pulled six encyclopedias from the bookcase and lugged them back to her bedroom. After placing them on the chair, she measured again: slightly over two feet. Perfect, Roseann thought.

Still in her robe and slippers, she climbed up onto the books and stood as tall as her five-foot-three-inch frame would let her. She reached up and easily touched the ceiling. Looking down, everything seemed to be miles away and out of perspective. Roseann reached down and discovered that she couldn't touch anything below her at that height. If she bent over slightly, she could touch the top of her lampshade. Reaching the surface of her nightstand that the lamp sat on was out of the question unless she bent way over. She tried it and nearly lost her balance.

Roseann stood back up and surveyed the room. It was dizzying, being so high above everything else. To her right, she could see the dust on top of her bookcase. And where did that scratch come from? She hadn't even known it was there! To her left, she was eye level with an Indiana University pennant that she had hung above a poster of Julie Andrews in *The Sound of Music*. She remembered climbing onto her desk chair to hang the pennant and poster.

Tossing her hair over her shoulders, Roseann turned to face the mirror over her dresser. It was a bizarre sight—all she could see of herself was from the chest down! Roseann stared at her headless image in the mirror.

"Jeez," she said out loud.

This is how Sandy Allen sees the world. It was an awesome thought. Her interview this morning should be very interesting.

Just then Scott poked his head in the door, which she had been unable to close all the way with her arms full of books.

"What are YOU doing?" he sneered, first looking up at his sister, then down at the encyclopedias beneath her pink fuzzy slippers.

Startled, Roseann wobbled a bit on the chair as she turned to look at him. "None of your business!" she replied. "Now get out of here, you little creep!" How embarrassing! She knew he'd talk about this forever.

"Man, what a weirdo," Scott said, shaking his head. He ducked back out of the door and continued down the hall to the bathroom. Relieved that he didn't demand further explanation, Roseann climbed down from the chair and put the books on her desk. She pushed all thoughts of her pesky brother out of her mind and tried to concentrate on the interview with Sandy, only a couple of hours away.

I'm going to make this the best article I've ever written, she determined.

14

Roseann pushed through the "in" door of the library, which was located in the center of the school's first floor. A desk separates that door from the "out" door on the other side: a setup designed to monitor the students' comings and goings, Roseann supposed. It was hard for her to picture the SHS library as a crime-ridden environment that required such policing. Most of the time, no one even sat at the checkout desk.

Roseann easily spotted Sandy Allen sitting at a table by herself in the back of the room. Even sitting down, Sandy stood out like a tall ship in a sea of tugboats. She was wearing a green dress that Roseann thought was much more flattering than some of her other clothes. Sandy's long legs were stretched out into the aisle and Roseann zeroed in on her feet. The hi-tops were gone, replaced by a pair of navy blue shoes made out of a suede-like material. Roseann was pleased at the possibility that Sandy had dressed up for the interview. Roseann herself had worn her new purple bell-bottom pants and her best white sweater.

Sandy looked up as Roseann approached and immediately drew her legs under the table.

"Hi," Roseann said cheerfully, placing her pile of books next to Sandy's on the long table just as the morning bell rang.

"Hello," Sandy replied. Her quiet, deep baritone sounded like a practiced library voice and Roseann gave her an "oops" smile. "I've never done an interview in a library before," she said in an apologetic whisper.

"I've never done an interview before," Sandy countered.

Roseann hoped Sandy's clever reply was a good sign that things would go well. She had so many questions to ask and figured it would take up the whole period.

I've done lots of interviews, she thought. Why do I feel edgy about this one?

Roseann quickly put her feelings aside and pulled out her notebook and pen. Sandy watched the procedure without emotion.

Roseann got out her list. "I guess I should start with the obvious question. How did you get to be so tall?" She flushed, immediately regretting the juvenile question. "I mean, I knew you grew that way, but is your height inherited, or what?"

"That's OK, everyone asks me that," Sandy answered, looking directly at the young reporter.

It was the first time Roseann could remember having eye contact with the girl. She usually kept her head bent or looked elsewhere. Even behind her black-rimmed glasses, Sandy had lovely eyes that complemented her dress.

"My family is normal-sized," Sandy said. "About six years ago I went to the Indiana University Medical Center in Indianapolis and a doctor there thought there was a tumor on my pituitary gland. That's where your growth hormone comes from. He wanted to do brain surgery on me, and I said no way."

"Brain surgery?" Roseann asked, confused.

"That's how you get to the pituitary," Sandy said, pointing to the back of her head. "It's at the base of the brain."

Roseann furiously wrote everything down, not wanting to miss a word. She had been ready for Sandy to say that her parents were extraordinarily tall, or that she had some seven-foot ancestor whose genes had been passed along to her. Roseann had heard of the pituitary gland but didn't know what its function was.

"How tall were you then?" she finally asked.

"Over six feet."

Roseann couldn't imagine a ten-year-old being the same size as a professional basketball player. It was unbelievable!

"How tall are you now?"

"I'm not exactly sure, but close to seven-foot-three."

Roseann tried to not visibly react to such a great height. "So," she began cautiously, "does that make you a . . . giant?"

"A giantess," Sandy corrected.

It was an exotic word. Roseann wrote it out and underlined it.

"So, if you don't have this surgery, you'll keep on growing?"

"I guess so," Sandy shrugged. "Actually, I have a syndrome called acromegaly. When the pituitary puts out too much growth hormone, it causes my hands and feet to enlarge and my internal organs swell up. It's also related to gigantism."

Sandy spelled acromegaly for Roseann, who was capturing every word. When she looked up from her notebook, she noticed that Sandy was a little pale.

"Are you OK?" Roseann asked.

"Sure," Sandy said, feeling herself break out into a sweat. "What else do you want to know?"

Roseann wasn't sure what to do. Should she pursue this medical angle, or ask her about the problems and advantages of her size like she had planned? Sandy was looking paler by the minute: Maybe it bothers her to talk about this surgery business, Roseann thought. Her curiosity about Sandy's medical issues won out.

"What did your parents think about your refusing the surgery?" Roseann ventured. "Did they want you to have it?"

Sandy hesitated, then looked down at the table. She reached out a large hand and ran her forefinger along the edge of her blue notebook. Roseann watched, her ballpoint pen poised above her notes.

"My parents are dead," Sandy said flatly. "I live with my grandmother and my little brother."

A pang of sympathy raced through Roseann. How awful, she thought. Not only did Sandy have to cope with her size, but she also had to deal with the loss of her parents. Roseann couldn't imagine what it would be like to not have her mom and dad around.

"I'm sorry. That must be really hard."

Sandy nodded in response, eyes still downcast.

"Have they . . . been gone long?" Roseann swallowed hard studying Sandy's broad face for some sign of emotion.

"A couple of years."

Roseann wrote that down. Her list of tall questions now seemed silly. She didn't want to upset Sandy, who was beginning to perspire. What do I do now? she thought. She hadn't expected this interview to go in such an unusual direction.

Roseann flipped the page in her spiral notebook to a clean sheet, filling time while trying to think. She was aware that Sandy was now watching her.

Two girls had come in the library and sat at the table across from them. They glanced at Sandy, then looked at each other and snickered. Roseann glared at them as they tried to suppress their silent but obvious laughter.

"How old is your brother?" she asked at last, turning back to the tall girl. If Sandy noticed the girls' rudeness, she didn't address it.

"Four. His name is Joey." Sandy didn't offer any more, but Roseann seized on this new, mutual ground.

"I have a little brother, too," Roseann said. "He's nine and a real pain,"

"I love my brother," Sandy replied matter-of-factly. "He's my whole life."

The large girl's tone was nonjudgmental, yet Roseann felt uncomfortable about her own remark about Scott. She knew he couldn't help doing half the stuff that he did to make her angry.

"What about your grandmother?" Roseann ventured. "Does she take care of both of you?"

Sandy perked up at the mention of Dora. "My granny is wonderful," Sandy told the red-haired girl. "She works real hard cleaning houses. She doesn't have much education, but she knows how to take care of us.

"She's a good seamstress, too," Sandy added. "She made the dress I have on. It isn't easy for me to buy clothes in stores."

"It's great. It goes well with your eyes."

Sandy blushed at the compliment. Perhaps no one had ever noticed her eyes before, let alone said anything nice about them.

"Thanks," she said. "I'll be getting new glasses soon." She seemed aware that Roseann was looking at them. "I hate these ugly things."

"Well, that will be good. It's hard to keep up with styles these days." Roseann wanted to be tactful.

"My granny makes most of my clothes." Sandy obviously was trying to steer the conversation away from her embarrassing glasses. Maybe they were the only kind of glasses she could afford on welfare, Roseann thought.

"Are all of your clothes special made?"

Sandy told Roseann about the Lane Bryant mail-order catalogues she used for some of her clothes. She ordered shoes from a men's catalogue—a size 16EEE that was still too small. She had to stuff her feet in them, she explained, unwinding her long legs from under the table and displaying her new shoes.

Sandy seemed comfortable talking about her clothes, and Roseann began to relax. Then they switched to basketball. Sandy told Roseann that she enjoyed the game, but she couldn't run as fast as she used to. Sandy had surgery when she was 14 to remove a tumor from her left knee, which was causing one side of her knee to grow faster than the other. She never quite regained the strength she had before, she said, and she had a second operation a year later in which doctors had to break bones and realign her kneecap with a metal plate and screws. Her knee still caused her some problems.

Then Sandy recalled a game in which the center on the other team tried to get the tip and Sandy turned to block her, causing the girl to come down hard on Sandy's back, tearing at her hair. Roseann winced.

"That must have hurt," she said.

"It hurt like hell," Sandy told her. "But I got the tip."

Roseann laughed out loud, then clamped her hand over her mouth. Mrs. Sherman, the librarian, looked up from her desk, staring at Roseann disapprovingly.

"Sorry," Roseann said in a loud whisper. A smile played at the corners of Sandy's mouth. Roseann grinned back at her.

"Don't worry about it, she won't say anything. She knows I'm the only one in here who can put books on the top shelf without a ladder," Sandy deadpanned.

Roseann choked back another laugh and bent over her notebook. She couldn't believe that this girl, who barely spoke to anyone, was joking about her height.

The rest of the interview went well for Roseann. Sandy made a couple of more jokes about screwing light bulbs into ceiling fixtures and putting the star on top of the Christmas tree without using a ladder. Only they weren't really jokes, Roseann discovered. Sandy really could do those things!

Sandy seemed to be happy enough answering Roseann's questions. Perhaps she could sense that the girl liked her. Probably a lot of people acted interested in Sandy because of her size, then they disappeared once their curiosity was satisfied.

Roseann watched as Sandy reached a large hand into her purse and pulled out a Kleenex. Sandy's long fingers pushed the tissue around and around in circles on her forehead, wadding the thin paper into a ball as it soaked up the perspiration.

Her mind flashed back to Delores, sitting in that hot tent with rivulets of sweat running down her face. The image loomed huge and dark in Roseann's mind, taunting her as she watched Sandy's Delores-sized hand swipe across her forehead. Even her expression of staid discomfort was like Delores's.

Roseann closed her eyes and shook her head to get rid of the image. When she opened them, Sandy was staring at the tabletop.

"Are you feeling OK?" Roseann asked.

"Just an upset stomach. It'll go away."

The sound of the dismissal bell startled them, and they gathered their books to leave. The girls across the aisle watched intently as Sandy stood up, towering over her companion.

Roseann glanced at them, then looked up at Sandy. She found she had to tilt her head back a ways to do that.

"Come on," she said, "I'll walk with you to the gym."

Roseann watched from behind as Sandy ducked her head going through the "out" door of the library, then fell in beside her in the hall. Her head, Roseann noticed, came just above Sandy's elbow. Sandy was glad to have someone to walk with, even though it was hard to carry on a conversation in the noisy hallway without bending over.

Suddenly, a group of boys came tearing around the corner. One of them crashed right into Sandy, sending her books flying all over the floor. Roseann watched in horror as Sandy lost her balance and fell against the lockers, her glasses clattering to the floor.

The boy recovered quickly as his friends stood there laughing.

"Look! It's the Jolly Green Giant!" one of them shouted.

"It's a monster!" yelled the long-haired boy who had run into her. "Oooooo! I probably have cooties now!" He made a face and danced around the hall, dramatically brushing off his clothes.

Roseann's heart pounded as she watched a laughing, jostling crowd gather, some of the kids singing the words to the old novelty tune called "The Jolly Green Giant." Several people just stared as they walked by.

Roseann's adrenalin raced as she looked over at Sandy, who was slumped against the lockers with her face away from everyone.

"Leave her alone!" Roseann screamed at the crowd.

"Ooooo, lookit the touchy redhead!" someone jeered. "Hey Red! You gonna get a green dress too?"

Roseann bristled, her face growing hot. "Shut up you jerk!" she shouted.

The boys looked at each other and whistled at the put-down. "Wow, Red's really got a mouth on her," said a tall, dark-haired boy with buck teeth.

Roseann ignored the comment, scanning the floor for Sandy's glasses. She scooped them up and discovered one of the temples had broken off. Panicked, she looked around but couldn't find it. She glanced at Sandy, who looked like she might cry.

Another girl had gathered Sandy's books and put them at her feet, walking away silently.

The boys pushed on past, still snickering. "You shouldn't scare people like that," one of them said to Sandy.

Sandy rose to her knees and picked up her books as Roseann rushed over to her.

"What a bunch of idiots!" Roseann steamed.

Sandy said nothing.

"Your glasses are broken. I'll try to find the other piece." Roseann searched both sides of the hallway but didn't find it. Those boys probably took it, she thought angrily.

"Well, I don't see it," she said out loud. She turned toward the tall girl just in time to see her several feet away, hurrying back toward the library.

"Sandy! Wait!" Roseann called, running after her.

Sandy turned the corner and Roseann got there just in time to see her go past the library toward the nurse's office.

Roseann opened her mouth to say something, then closed it. She looked down at Sandy's broken glasses in her hand, then at her watch. Only a minute until the bell and she had to dress out for gym.

What should she do? The hallways were emptying, and she didn't think Sandy wanted to be followed. Especially if she was going to be sick.

Roseann felt sick herself as she walked back to where she had dumped her own books on the floor. Dejected, she picked them up, still holding Sandy's black-framed glasses in her hand. Underneath her books lay the missing piece she had been looking for.

Roseann was relieved. Well, she thought, carefully putting the glasses into her purse, I'll just give them to her later.

She broke into a run and got to the locker room just under the bell. Allison, the girl who had befriended Roseann the first day of school, was at the bench, bent over and tying her shoes.

"Did you have a good interview?" she asked cheerfully as Roseann worked her locker combination.

"Yeah," she replied. "Just great."

15

Sandy didn't show up for gym class. Roseann kept stealing glances toward the locker room door, hoping to see the girl she'd just interviewed come in late. She had a hard time concentrating on the volleyball rules they were learning because her mind kept picturing the incident in the hallway and the humiliation that Sandy must have felt. Roseann wished she could check up on her somehow.

When Sandy wasn't at her usual table at lunch, Roseann decided she had probably gone home. It's so unfair, Roseann thought. The girl hadn't done anything to anyone, yet she was treated so cruelly. Then she thought about her own outburst, and how she had put herself on the line for a girl she barely knew. She should be embarrassed, she thought—it certainly was the wrong way to make an impression at SHS. Still, she felt pretty good about it. Doing that at her old school would have been out of the question. It was not cool to befriend kids who were unpopular or "different."

Roseann wasn't really hungry but grabbed a ham sandwich and a carton of milk anyway. She didn't feel sociable and decided to just go over her interview notes during lunch. Turning from the cash register, she saw Julie Jackson waving at her and pointing to an empty chair at her table. Roseann sighed and made her way across the room, halfway glad for the attention but preferring to eat alone.

As usual, Julie was carrying on a vivacious conversation with her friends, Sarah and Mary Anne, whom Roseann had eaten lunch with before. Sarah's greatest ambition was to get married and have four kids – two boys and two girls. Mary Anne had her sights set on Hollywood.

She wanted to be an actress and meet Doris Day, Carol Burnett and all her other favorite stars. They were nice girls and Roseann liked them.

Roseann said hi to everyone as she set her books and tray down. The trio looked up at her with interest.

"So," Julie said, turning toward Roseann with a smile. "How'd your interview go? I didn't have a chance to ask you last hour."

"Fine," Roseann replied cautiously, not really wanting to talk about it. "I should have the story done in a couple of weeks."

"Great," Julie responded with a grin, showing the slight gap between her two front teeth. "I can't wait to read it." Sarah and Mary Anne nodded in agreement.

Roseann felt a prickle of pleased embarrassment run down her neck. Julie always seemed to be sincere no matter how much she joked around.

Suddenly, Julie leaned over to Roseann and whispered, "Come with me to the john."

Roseann looked at her quizzically, then picked up her purse and followed the dark-haired girl out of the cafeteria. They ducked into the nearest restroom and Roseann suppressed a smile as she watched Julie bend down and check under the stalls for feet. No feet; that was good.

"What happened in the hallway today?" Julie asked while hauling herself up from the floor. She looked concerned. "Sarah and Mary Anne were just telling me about it."

Roseann rolled her eyes. "Is this all over the school or something?"

"It will be by the end of the day," Julie said matter-of-factly. "That doesn't say much for news value around here, does it."

Roseann offered a half-smile. She told Julie what had happened to Sandy Allen in the hall and how Sandy just sat there, taking the abuse, until Roseann could no longer stand it.

"What did you do?" Julie asked, pulling out a pack of Juicy Fruit and offering Roseann a stick.

"Told them to leave her alone," Roseann related, accepting the gum. "Called some guy a jerk. I wanted to call him something worse," she added.

"Yeah?" Julie grinned. "Way to go, Bellamy!"

"Well, I certainly made my mark at SHS today, I guess."

"Hey, it's no big wazoo. Besides," Julie switched to a serious tone, "this may be just the thing you need to give your article some depth, depending on what angle you're taking. Think about it."

Roseann looked down at the piece of gum, which she had rolled into a ball, then put it in her mouth. Julie had just presented her with an interesting thought! Could she turn the unfortunate hallway experience into something positive? A nagging thought crossed her mind. She and Julie looked at each other silently for a few moments before she spoke.

"I wouldn't want to do or say anything at Sandy's expense," she said finally.

Julie nodded. Was she being a good editor? Or a friend?

"You'll figure it out," Julie said encouragingly.

Roseann sighed. She had never been involved in a story that had so many different—and confusing—aspects.

"And don't worry about that deal in the hallway. In a couple of days, the whole thing will be history."

"I hope you're right. But more for her sake than mine."

Julie gave her a sympathetic smile. "Come on," she said, walking toward the door. "Let's chow."

16

By the end of the day, Roseann felt depressed. She was still carrying around Sandy's glasses and wondered how she was going to get along without them. Should she call Sandy? Maybe deliver them to her house? She was sure her mom or dad would drive her there. She needed to talk to Mom, she thought, suddenly anxious to get away from the home of the Golden Bears.

Barbara Bellamy was on the front porch this crisp October afternoon, rearranging crysanthemum pots when Roseann got home. It was a large porch that wrapped halfway around the older, two-story house that was similar to others on their block. Tall trees dipped their branches toward the gabled roof where Roseann's bedroom was, looking strong and protective.

When they had first moved to Shelbyville, Roseann despised their new house. She was used to the sprawling brick ranch that had been her home since she was five. No one had big porches in her neighborhood, but there were backyard patios—and sometimes swimming pools—like Ashley's. She had looked at the new place and groaned.

Now, the porch looked friendly and inviting, especially with her mother there, squatting on the floor in her bell-bottom jeans and an Indiana University sweatshirt. She looked young, her dark hair pulled back with a couple of Roseann's hair clips.

"Hi, Mom," she said, parking herself on the top step and plunking her books on the porch. "Where's Scott?" Somewhere else, she hoped.

"Hey, sweetie." Mrs. Bellamy turned, still on her knees, showing a dirt-smudged cheek. "What's up?"

"Is Scott around? I need to talk to you."

"He's down the street somewhere. Far out of earshot," her mother said, giving Roseann a knowing smile. She scooted across the gray floor on her rear, leaning her back against the railing post across from her daughter.

Mom always knew what she was thinking, Roseann noticed. Sometimes it unnerved her, but mostly it was a comfortable feeling, like they shared a special secret.

"Did something happen at school?" her mother pressed.

"Sort of. I mean, yes."

Roseann launched into the whole story about Sandy Allen and the interview and the incident with the boys in the hallway. She knew she was laying a lot on her mom—this was the first time she had ever mentioned Sandy—but they hadn't had much time to talk lately. Roseann felt grateful for this brisk, fall day and her mother's undivided attention.

She finished it by saying she had yelled at the perpetrators and they had laughed at her.

Mrs. Bellamy listened intently to Roseann's story about Sandy, which sounded kind of junior high-ish in the retelling.

"Do you think you did the right thing?" Mrs. Bellamy looked squarely at Roseann.

Roseann looked down at the porch. "Yes," she said. "And I'd do it again." Once she said it, she realized her convictions. She hadn't felt strongly about anything for a long time. Her motivations, though, seemed clouded.

"Roseann," said Mrs. Bellamy, "there are a lot of cruel people in this world. In high school, at the hospital where your dad works—everywhere. Kids are under a lot of pressure to conform, and anyone who's different is an easy target.

"Obviously, these kids have found a very vulnerable target in Sandy," she went on. "She doesn't fight back. Kids that tease someone like that are insecure about themselves. Making fun of someone is a cover-up for their own lack of self-esteem. Sometimes they have to make someone else look bad to make themselves look good."

"That's a cop-out," Roseann said indignantly.

"That's right, it is. I'm glad you recognize it, and I'm proud of you for standing up for her."

"Even if I called that guy a jerk?"

"Well," said Mrs. Bellamy, raising an eyebrow, "some people do strange things under duress. I think that, in some way, you were standing up for the person who couldn't stand up for herself."

Roseann grinned. Barbara Bellamy was cool when it came to understanding her kids' behavior. Even Scott's. Did the kids at his school tease him because he acts different sometimes? She didn't even know.

Roseann sighed. "Thanks, Mom," she said. "I just don't know what to do to help Sandy, other than writing this story and hope people will be able to see her differently."

"It's a start. The most important thing you can do is try to be her friend."

Roseann pondered that a bit. Did she actually want to be friends with Sandy? Was that possible, considering that the girl was such a loner? There were still a lot of mysterious things about her that Roseann didn't know, even after talking to her.

I wonder what it would be like, she thought, being friends with the school outcast.

Roseann stood up and bent over to retrieve her books, her red hair swinging in her face. She leaned over and kissed her mother right on the dirt smudge. "I'll try, Mom. Thanks," she said. Mrs. Bellamy smiled after her daughter as the girl shifted her books and yanked open the screen door with her free hand.

"By the way," Mrs. Bellamy called after her, "there's a letter from Ashley on the hall table."

17

Roseann bounded down the steps of the school bus the next morning and hurried through the front door of the sandstone-colored Shelbyville High School building. She angled to the left, consciously avoiding the emblem on the floor—in case the Senior Emblem Police were watching—and headed straight for the library. Sandy Allen's glasses were tucked safely away in her purse. She had fixed them the night before by taking the hinge pin out of an old pair of sunglasses to replace the one missing in Sandy's, and secured it with black electricians tape. It barely showed at all on the black frames.

She was worried that Sandy might not show up at school today but was relieved to find her shelving books in the reference section of the library. Sandy didn't see her approach, and Roseann had to tap her on the elbow to get her attention. She noticed a large bruise on Sandy's forearm, the one that had gotten squashed into the lockers.

"Hi. How are you feeling today?" Roseann inquired.

Sandy seemed startled to see Roseann there. It took her a few seconds to respond, then said, "Much better."

"Did you go home early?"

Sandy nodded.

"Are you . . . hurt?"

Sandy subconsciously put her hand over the bruise. But even her large hand couldn't completely cover it. "I'm fine," she said stoically. Roseann saw she had dark circles under her eyes.

Roseann reached into her purse and pulled out Sandy's glasses, which she had wrapped in tissue paper, and handed them to her.

"I tried to fix them," she said. "I hope they're OK."

Sandy accepted them silently and put them on. "Thanks," she said, looking somewhat embarrassed. "You didn't have to do that."

Roseann smiled, slightly embarrassed herself. She wanted to say something significant to Sandy, something that would reassure her that everything would be all right, but the words wouldn't come. Maybe things wouldn't be all right. They certainly weren't for Delores Pullard.

"Listen," she said, looking at Sandy earnestly, "those guys were such morons."

Sandy shrugged. "Morons are a big part of my life."

Roseann didn't have a response to that: She was finding out every day that Sandy was right.

"I need to get to my locker before the bell," Roseann said. "I'll see you in gym, OK?"

Sandy nodded, eyes downcast. "Thanks again for my glasses," she offered. She looked like she wanted to say something else, but didn't.

"No problem," Roseann replied with a smile. She turned and walked toward the library door, then glanced back at Sandy before opening it.

The girl was standing there against a background of books, staring across the room at Roseann.

The English wing was on the other side of the school from the gym, and Roseann always had to run to get to journalism class before the bell rang. Usually her hair was still damp from the shower—she pinned it up so it didn't get totally wet—and she felt half put-together by the time she arrived. She was grateful for Tuesdays and Thursdays, though, when she reported directly to the *Courier* office. Mrs. Musgrave was usually in class and didn't make an appearance for a while, so most of the newspaper kids strolled in late. So much for prompt attendance.

Today, Roseann was halfway up the stairs when the bell rang. She was planning to use the whole period to organize her Sandy Allen story, which she had been thinking about on and off all day. Please let there be a typewriter available, she thought as she opened the door to the *Courier* office.

Randy Kozlowski, the senior editor, looked up from his desk as Roseann walked in. He was tall and blond, his hair long like most of the boys wore it these days, but not as shaggy. He had one of the most dazzling smiles Roseann had ever seen, which he offered to her as she entered the room.

"Hi," he said. "You're Roseann, right?"

"Guilty," she replied, putting her books on the desk near the door. No one else was in the room, which was barely big enough for two people anyway.

"I'm Randy," he offered.

"I know. You're the senior editor." He was looking at her with interest and suddenly she felt very shy.

"Guilty," he said with a laugh.

Roseann smiled. At least he has a sense of humor, which is more she could say for the other guys in this school.

"Mrs. Musgrave tells me that your strong area is people, that you like to do personality profiles."

Roseann thought about saying "guilty" but chucked the idea as being too cute. "It's what I enjoy most," she said instead. "I'm doing a story on Sandy Allen."

Randy gave her another smile and raised his eyebrows.

"The tall girl? That should be interesting."

Roseann nodded and asked if she could use one of the two typewriters in the office.

"Sure, go ahead. Everyone else is off doing whatever today. I thought I was going to be in here alone, but I'm glad you came along."

Roseann felt herself blush.

"But before you get started, I have an assignment for you," he added in a more serious tone. "The fall musical this year is My Fair Lady and I'd like you to interview the female lead, Brenda Smart. We can set something up next week during rehearsals after school."

Roseann knew who Brenda Smart was—a thin and pretty girl who was Shelbyville High's major talent. She was in Roseann's Spanish class.

"Sounds great," said Roseann.

"I think you'll enjoy it—she's pretty colorful," said Randy, offering Roseann another of his trademark smiles.

Roseann spent the weekend finishing the Sandy Allen piece at home on her old Royal typewriter. It was pretty long—five pages, double spaced—but Julie said the length would be OK. With no friends to hang out with, Roseann's weekends were filled with reading or puttering around her room, rearranging her collections and children's books.

Sometimes she took long walks around the west side of town where she lived, acknowledging the beauty of the tree-laden streets but not really feeling connected to them. Even though things were looking up at school, Shelbyville was still foreign land to her; a territory to explore, but not become a part of. Her heart was in Indianapolis, with its widely spaced houses and the kids she grew up with.

She did have something to look forward to: Her letter last week from Ashley had been an invitation to spend next Saturday night at her slumber party to celebrate her 16th birthday. Roseann could hardly wait to see her old friends!

The following Tuesday, Julie came banging through the *Courier* office door, trying to juggle a large stack of books which was tipping precariously. Roseann leaped up to grab some of them, but it was too late—half of them went crashing to the floor.

"Darn," Julie mumbled, slamming the rest of the stack onto a desk. Roseann dove for the floor and gathered up the fallen books, which were old English texts, and put them next to the other stack.

"Thanks," said Julie, wiping her hands on her jeans. "Can you believe it? Musgrave wants us to save these suckers, and they haven't been used for years! That woman saves EVERYTHING. And she thinks there's room HERE in this glorified Port-a-Potty."

Roseann grinned at the brown-eyed girl, who stuck out her lower jaw to blow the hair out of her eyes. It usually just flopped right back where it was, but she always did it anyway.

"How about on top of the file cabinet?" Roseann suggested, reaching for the stack she had just put down. Julie nodded, and they shoved the books back against the wall on top of the gray metal cabinet.

After Julie had settled into one of the three chairs in the room, Roseann tentatively handed her the folder with her story on Sandy. Suddenly, she felt self-conscious and wondered if it was as good as she had thought it was.

"I finished this last night," she said a bit nervously. "Do you have time to take a look at it?"

Julie pulled out Roseann's copy and propped her feet up on the desk. She was wearing old sneakers that had a hole on one side, with a pink sock showing through. Roseann stared at it, then looked away.

"I love your title!" Julie was saying. "*The Weather Up Here Is Fine.* That's super."

Roseann smiled. She nervously ran her fingers around the keys of the beat-up manual typewriter on the desk in front of her while Julie read. By the time Julie got to the second page, she was looking pleased, and Roseann relaxed a little.

"This is great, very sensitive approach but with humor, too. It really makes Sandy seem less mysterious," Julie pointed out. "There are things in here that I didn't know about her, and I've known her since kindergarten."

Roseann felt goosebumps rising on her arms. It was exactly what she had hoped to get across about the unusual girl. She didn't know what to say, but Julie didn't seem to expect a reply. After the third page, Julie stopped reading and put the pages back in order, then returned them to the folder.

"I have some other stuff to do so I'll have to finish this later," she said. "Then I'll show it to Musgrave, and she'll discuss any changes with you. Then we can work on the layout and have a photo taken of Sandy, OK?"

"Yes. Thanks," said Roseann. She felt very pleased with herself and her first story for the *Courier*.

She heard a noise behind her and turned to see Randy Kozlowski coming through the door with another stack of books. His long blond hair was hanging in his face and he tilted his head to the side so he could see.

"She got you too, huh?" Julie laughed, pointing to the top of the file cabinet.

"Yeah. Hi, Roseann," he said, grinning at her.

Julie raised an eyebrow in her direction, and Roseann felt her face flush.

Randy busied himself with the books, then pulled out a file drawer and rummaged through some folders.

"Here's some homework on Brenda Smart," he said, closing the drawer. His blue eyes, half-hidden behind the shock of hair, were look-ing right into hers. "Just put them back in the folder marked 'music' when you're done."

"Uh, thanks," Roseann managed. Out of the corner of her eye, she could see Julie watching with interest. An awkward silence fol-lowed, then Randy brushed past her to go out the door.

"More books," he said apologetically. "Musgrave's on a cleaning binge."

"Have fun," she called after him. The comment came easily, as if she were talking to someone she knew real well. Inwardly, it startled her a bit, as if she had let down her guard against liking something about SHS.

"Do you think he's cute?" Julie asked. She bent over and retied her holey sneaker.

"Well, sure, don't you?"

Julie nodded. "Me and every third girl in this school," she said, standing up. "I'm going to see if Randy needs any help hauling books. Want to come?"

Roseann shook her head no. "I need to read these clips," she said.

"Well," Julie said lightly, whacking Roseann on the head with the folder, "between Sandy and Brenda Smart, you will have hit the two most eccentric people in the whole school."

Roseann looked after her, wondering what she meant. Then she spread out the clippings and began to read.

18

On the following Monday, Sandy Allen had been at her usual table in the cafeteria, staring at a bowl of chili. One of the few times she decided to go through the hot lunch line, and she didn't feel like eating. If I do, she thought, it will just come right back up again.

The cafeteria noise buzzed loudly around her, but she was too lost in her own thoughts to pay any attention to it. She reached for a potato chip, took it delicately between her fingers and poked it into her mouth.

Last night, Violet had gone on another rampage, pulling out drawers all over the house and dumping them on the floor. Someone had thrown out an incomplete deck of cards—probably Dora—and Vi had found them in the trash.

"These are my drawers," she screamed. "No one takes my things out of my drawers!"

"What good is part of a deck of cards?" Sandy shouted back, knowing it would just provoke her. She didn't care. She was still seething over the axed bicycle incident.

Joey had run into the bathroom, where he usually went when Vi was acting out, and shut the door.

Violet narrowed her eyes, "You think you're so smart," she challenged the tall girl. "Well, you don't know bull!"

"I know you. Same thing," Sandy countered.

Violet had picked up a knife from the overturned silverware drawer and raised it over her head toward Sandy. It was a regular table knife and Sandy almost laughed.

"You couldn't stab hot butter with that thing," Sandy announced smugly. No matter how much Violet threatened Sandy, she had never laid a hand on her. But Sandy knew she'd take it out on Joey, so she backed off.

"Just put that down and let's clean this mess up before Granny gets home," Sandy suggested reasonably.

Violet lowered the knife and frowned at Sandy. She looked defeated, as if she had forgotten why she was mad. That happened a lot with her. Sandy thought she ought to be locked up.

Now Sandy brought a spoonful of chili to her mouth, then she put it down again. No way, she thought, feeling the acid from her stomach crawling up into her throat. She pushed herself out of the tiny, orange cafeteria chair and stood her full height, causing several kids at surrounding tables to look up at her. She gathered her books under one arm and headed for the tray return, where she dumped her untouched lunch into the trash.

Then she loped out of the cafeteria and down the hall toward the south wing for her usual lunchtime ritual. That is how Roseann had seen her, desperate but stoic, unable to share her problems.

•   •   •   •   •

Roseann watched Sandy Allen leave the cafeteria, ducking her head as she went through the doorway. Every day, Roseann noticed, Sandy leaves the lunchroom early. Maybe the stares and comments get to her, she thought. Maybe she goes to the library to study—she seems to feel safe in there.

Sandy had sat out gym period that day. Apparently she wasn't feeling well.

Even though Mary Anne had waved her over to the table she shared with Julie and Sarah, Roseann was sitting by herself, cramming for her Spanish test that afternoon. Her ham and swiss sandwich tasted all right but she wasn't very hungry. She closed her Spanish book and decided to find Sandy and give her a copy of the story she had written about her, as promised.

She dumped her tray, then headed out of the cafeteria in the same direction Sandy went. Roseann followed the hallway to the library and entered the "in" door. Glancing around the room, she didn't see Sandy anywhere. Sandy was easy to spot, Roseann thought with amusement. Even Sandy had said so.

Coming out of the library, Roseann turned toward the offices and the lobby. Then, down the next hallway that led to the math rooms, she saw the giant figure in blue slacks, hunched over a pay phone. Sandy was bent over so far that, from that angle, Roseann couldn't even see her head.

Who's she talking to? Roseann wondered. Intuitively, she felt as if Sandy was in some kind of trouble. Maybe that's just the way it is with loners. Roseann didn't know. But she wished she could find out.

That same afternoon in English class, Roseann gave Sandy a copy of the newspaper article and told her to look it over, and if there was something that needed to be changed or clarified, to let her know. Sandy returned it the next day, saying it was fine, but made no specific comments, which disappointed Roseann. She had hoped Sandy would be really pleased about the article, which she felt was well-balanced between the good and bad of being her size. She explained acromegaly and how it affected Sandy. Other than saying her parents were deceased and that she was living with her grandmother, Roseann didn't dwell too much on her family. She felt that was too personal.

On Thursday during her newspaper class, she did a little bit of re-writing and doublechecked her spelling. Randy Kozlowski, the senior editor, wasn't in that day, but Julie Jackson was. Roseann asked Julie if she'd finish looking it over before it was turned in to Mrs. Musgrave, and Julie said she would assign a photographer to take a couple of photos of Sandy in the library to go with the story.

Roseann finally felt that she had accomplished something at Shelbyville High.

19

The following Wednesday, as Roseann headed toward her journalism class, Julie Jackson came charging down the hallway toward her.

"I have to talk to you," she said breathlessly, grabbing Roseann's elbow and pulling her toward the lockers on the other side of the hall.

"What's up?" Roseann asked. Julie did not look happy.

Julie stopped a moment to catch her breath. She set her books on the floor, then pulled out the folder containing the article on Sandy from the pile.

"There's a problem with your article," she said, leafing through the story to page four. Roseann looked at her expectantly. What could possibly be wrong with it?

Julie ran her hand through her hair, then leaned conspiratorially toward Roseann, who looked over her shoulder at the copy.

"Here," Julie said, pointing to the center of the page. "You've quoted Sandy as saying that her parents are dead and she is living with her grandmother. Is that what she said?"

"Yeah, why?" Roseann frowned. Did Julie think she couldn't get a simple quote right?

"Her mother isn't dead, she just left," Julie informed her. "My mom knows the family. Sandy lives with her aunt, grandmother and brother about six blocks from me. Her aunt is meaner than an alligator with a toothache. She probably didn't want to tell you that."

Humiliation filled Roseann right down to her toes. Her first story and there already was a problem! She had felt so sorry for Sandy because her parents were dead. Now Sandy had put the young writer's integrity on the line.

"Thanks," Roseann mumbled, shoving the folder under her history book. "I'll take care of it."

"Sorry," Julie said, giving Roseann a sympathetic look. She picked up her books and walked into the classroom just as the bell rang, leaving Roseann standing in the hall.

Mrs. Musgrave stood in front of the journalism class lecturing about protecting confidential sources in news stories.

"Some reporters have gone to jail for refusing to reveal their sources," she was saying, her dimples appearing and disappearing into her cheeks as she talked. Roseann had trouble concentrating. Her mind kept wandering back to Sandy Allen and the deception about her parents and aunt. Sandy knew the story would be in the *Courier*. What made her think she could get away with such a lie, especially since some of her classmates probably knew the truth.

Roseann didn't know what to do. Should she confront Sandy during lunch? Should she just forget talking to Sandy and leave that information out of the story?

Someone tapped Roseann on the shoulder, and Roseann turned partway around in her seat. The boy behind her handed her a note that was folded into a small square. She opened it and found it was from Julie, who sat a couple of seats behind her in the next row.

"Don't talk to Sandy yet," it said in Julie's squiggly handwriting. "Can you come over to my apt. after school Friday night? I have something important to show you." At the bottom of the note she had drawn a map showing the center part of town, with an X marking the location of her apartment building and the address. Perplexed, Roseann refolded the note and stuck it in her purse. She turned around and glanced at Julie, who was looking right at her for an answer. Roseann nodded yes.

I wonder what this is all about? she thought.

20

The SHS lobby was filled with kids wearing peace symbol buttons and holding anti-war signs that said "War is dangerous to children and other living things." It was Friday afternoon when Roseann was scheduled to interview Brenda Smart, who was in rehearsals for the fall musical, *My Fair Lady*. Everyone had been talking about the peace rally all week, and the lobby swelled with what looked like half the school.

Vietnam was an unpopular war but a very popular topic these days. High school kids were staging mini-protests, taking a cue from college students who were demonstrating on campuses across the country.

On one side of the room, a group of kids was gathered around a girl playing the guitar and singing "Abraham, Martin and John." Several teachers and administrators stood around looking nervous. A rally on school grounds—unless it was a school-sanctioned event—was against policy. Apparently, it was going to be allowed as long as everyone behaved properly.

Roseann looked toward the two sets of doors that led to Breck Auditorium just off the lobby. All of them were blocked by kids. Over to one side stood Randy Kozlowski, leaning against the wall with his hands in his pockets. He seemed to be by himself. Roseann waved at him but he didn't look her way.

To her left she spotted Julie Jackson, who was wearing long, dangly earrings shaped like peace symbols and a pink tie-dyed shirt. Roseann caught her eye, and Julie waved her over.

"Pretty good turnout, huh?" Julie commented. "Hey, you look

pretty dressed-up for the occasion."

Roseann looked down at her black mini-skirt, purple sweater and black go-go boots, which felt hot on her legs, but looked great with a mini. She always dressed up for an interview; it made her feel more professional and self-confident.

"I have an interview with Brenda Smart today," she explained. "She's in rehearsal. All I have to do is figure out how to get through the door," she added, looking toward the auditorium, which was blocked by a sea of reclining denim. Randy was still standing by himself over to one side of the doors.

"I see Randy over there," Roseann pointed out. "Is he covering this for the *Courier?*"

Julie gave her a wan smile. "No, he asked Barry Newkirk to do it. He's over there with a camera."

Roseann looked where Julie was pointing and saw Barry, who was both staff photographer and a senior reporter, focusing his Nikon on the kids with the guitar.

Roseann's puzzlement showed, and Julie took her arm and pulled her closer.

"Randy's brother was killed in Vietnam last year," she said quietly. "I don't think he feels that he can cover something like this objectively."

Roseann felt a chill go up her spine. Even in Indianapolis, she didn't know anyone whose family had had a Vietnam casualty.

"That's awful," she finally said.

"Yeah," said Julie. "It was really hard on him. He and his brother were close."

Roseann didn't know what to say. "I've gotta go," she said abruptly. "See you later."

Roseann made her way across the lobby, stepping over outstretched legs and trying not to let any of the boys look up her skirt. As she approached the auditorium doors, she noticed Randy watching her. Roseann smiled at him self-consciously, and Randy nodded back at her. Then he pulled his hand out of his pocket and gave her the two-finger peace sign.

She shifted her books onto her left arm and returned the sign. A group of kids scooted over enough for her to pass, and with one last glance at Randy, she grabbed the handle and gave the heavy auditorium door a pull.

Roseann stepped inside the auditorium and closed the door quietly. Brenda Smart and the male lead—she'd have to remember to get his name later—were standing by the piano looking at sheet music with Dave Wallant, the head of the school's music department.

Breck Auditorium wasn't quite as big as the one at North Central, but it was just as impressive, she thought, looking around at the bright red seats and a stage framed with gold and black curtains. Roseann felt the stress of her day lifting as she took in the majesty of the room: There was something thrilling about the theater that had captured Roseann at an early age. Being in an auditorium had always held a certain magic for her—an escape into a world full of spine-tingling music and talented performers who could transform an ordinary stage into another world.

Roseann took a seat about halfway down and focused on what was happening on the stage. Brenda, a tall brunette with curly hair, had found her mark on the floor and was waiting patiently while Mr. Wallant explained something to the boy who was playing Henry Higgins, the aristocrat who took in Eliza Doolittle, the poor flower vendor, and tried to civilize her.

They rehearsed "The Rain in Spain," one of the show's light numbers, transforming themselves into their characters as Roseann watched delightedly. The boy was singing from sheet music, but Brenda was strutting and posturing around the stage, singing all the words from memory in a perfect Cockney accent. Henry Higgins was having a hard time trying not to laugh at the wide-eyed Eliza that Brenda had created, a character whose comic timing had to be just right—innocently funny, but not too hammy. Brenda seemed to know just when to pull back.

Roseann watched, fascinated. The girl's performance was every bit as good as those she had seen at Starlight Musicals, an outdoor theater in Indianapolis, and that was professional theater! Brenda's voice was strong, and she had a commanding presence on stage. Roseann knew she was watching someone who was extraordinarily gifted.

After rehearsal, Brenda came down to where Roseann was sitting, introducing herself with a firm handshake.

"You're really terrific," Roseann told her.

"Thank you." Brenda's speaking voice was as pleasant as her singing voice.

The interview went very well, and Roseann was fascinated by the young girl whose aspirations included getting out of Shelbyville and possibly going to New York to study voice and acting. Brenda was very self-assured without being arrogant. She obviously had her eye on the prize—Broadway—and was going to go after it. A colorful speaker, she gave Roseann some good quotes, always a reporter's dream. This will be a fun story to write, Roseann thought.

Eventually, Brenda turned the tables on the young reporter and started asking Roseann questions about herself: where she was from and what she wanted to do with her life. Roseann was pleased with her interest. When she asked what stories Roseann had written, Roseann hesitated, then found herself telling Brenda the whole story about Sandy's interview and how embarrassed she was when her editor discovered the reference to Sandy's parents being dead. She said she wasn't sure how to handle it and had thought about confronting Sandy about her lie.

"Well," Brenda said, rolling her eyes, "if I had a crazy person in the house I wouldn't want anyone to know about it either."

"What?" Roseann looked at Brenda intently. Julie had said the aunt was mean, but crazy too?

"Her aunt is looney-tunes. She's loud and drunk most of the time, kind of the town joke," Brenda explained. "Go easy on Sandy—she had good reason to say what she did. I don't imagine her home life is a bed of roses."

Roseann was stunned. "I didn't know," she said quietly.

"How could you? You did the interview in good faith. Heck, I could be lying to you, too."

Roseann offered the girl a half-smile. "If you are, you're a better

74

actress than I thought," she said.

Brenda laughed appreciatively. "Touché," she replied. "Listen, it'll work out."

Roseann smiled gratefully. She couldn't believe that she not only had found someone at SHS who shared her feelings about the school and the town, but also had given her some insight into Sandy Allen's behavior.

21

Sandy sat bolt upright, swiping her hand across her brow and flinging her arm out to the side of the bed. It was quiet in the house and she heard the water bug hit the floor—the third one that had crawled across her face that night. She knew that she should be used to them by now, but they continued to terrify her.

Her heart was pounding as she carefully lay back down, trying not to wake Dora, who had stirred when Sandy moved. As her eyes adjusted to the dark, she turned her head to read the clock on the dresser. It was a little after 4 a.m., and she had to get up in an hour for basketball practice.

She knew that going back to sleep was impossible.

Sandy put her hands behind her head, hoping that her arms would stop any more of the bugs from getting close to her face. Thank God it was getting cooler outside, she thought. The water bugs would soon disappear for the winter. She had spent much of the summer sitting up all night, reading, afraid to go to bed. When morning came and the bugs scurried out of sight, Sandy was able to sleep. She got into the habit of shaking out her shoes and clothes before putting them on. Once, Dora had come to bed with a water bug clinging to the back of her nightgown. Sandy had swatted it so hard that it smashed against the wall.

Maybe the bugs would carry Violet off with them, she thought dryly. The night before, Violet had screamed at Joey for some minor offense, then had turned on Dora for defending him. She didn't quiet down until Sandy intervened. Sandy didn't know how much longer she could deal with Violet's unpredictable behavior. Just the other day Violet had chased the boy over to a neighbor's house with a knife. Sandy had to go and get him when she came home from school.

It was bad enough to have her mother desert her, she thought, but to have this stranger, who thought she was in charge, boss them around—what a mess. Why did this terrible woman have to be with them, anyway? It was true that Dora couldn't raise Joey and her too —it was the welfare money that she needed—but this was an impossible situation.

Sandy stretched her body out to its full length until her lower legs and feet hung over the end of the bed, feeling the aches that had settled into her bones during the night. She looked forward to warming up in the gym each morning: It limbered up her body and gave her energy. Something nagged at her, though. After her leg surgery, it was getting harder and harder to run down the court. She wondered how effective she was on the team.

Sandy sighed wearily. She felt tired: tired and trapped within the walls of the tiny, cluttered house. Life and all of its burdens pressed heavily on her, smothering her, making her feel old. One of these days, she thought, I'm not going to be able to hold my temper. Then there's no telling what I'll do to keep Joey safe.

•   •   •   •   •

Roseann stuck Julie's map into the pocket of her jeans and headed up Washington Street toward town. Just like Indianapolis, Shelbyville had a landscaped Circle, which you could drive around, to mark the center of town. But Indy's Circle was much bigger, with the towering Soldiers and Sailors Monument as its anchor. You could climb all the way to the top of it by stairway, or take an elevator to get a great view of the downtown area. Shelbyville's park-like center was pleasant but unimpressive. Oh well, thought Roseann, at least she could walk the streets here and feel relatively safe.

She wondered what Julie had to show her, and why she was making such a mystery of it. She hadn't mentioned it in class or at lunch for the last two days, other than reconfirming that Roseann would be there. It was the first time anyone in Shelbyville had invited her anywhere, and she jumped at the chance no matter what the reason. Besides, she enjoyed Julie's company.

As she approached the main part of town, she located the small, two-story apartment building, sandwiched between a restaurant and a dime store. Roseann couldn't remember the last time she had seen a dime store and made a mental note to explore it sometime.

The apartment building was old, constructed of gray cement block, with a dark red front door that opened right onto the sidewalk. It was a plain building, boxy-looking but solid.

Roseann squared her shoulders and pulled open the door, which led into a hallway dimly lit by one ceiling light. To her right were eight mailboxes with names taped to them. As Julie had instructed, Roseann climbed the stairway to the second floor and looked for apartment G, which was located in the front of the building. The stairs were covered with fairly new-looking, indoor-outdoor carpeting in earth tone stripes, which ended at the top step. Scarred dark green tile covered the hallway floor. The walls, whose color had faded to a ghastly shade of greenish-yellow, were covered with graffiti. Gross, Roseann thought.

There was a door knocker on apartment G and Roseann tapped it gingerly three times. "I'll get it!" she heard Julie shout from inside.

"Hi!" she said, flinging the door open. "Come on in." Julie seemed to be genuinely glad to see her new friend. Roseann returned the greeting and followed her through the door, which opened into a small sitting room. It had dark paneled walls filled with pictures of Elvis Presley in karate poses and from his TV concert special, *Aloha From Hawaii*. One was a very large velvet portrait like the kind Roseann had seen at flea markets.

"As you can see, our decorator is out to lunch," Julie said, waving a hand toward the Elvis gallery. Roseann smiled at the joke but didn't say anything.

"I heard that," said a giggly voice from the next room. The girls entered a much larger room that took up the whole front of the apartment, with a high ceiling and a row of tall windows. A short, square-faced woman wearing bell-bottom pants and a black Elvis T-shirt stood grinning by the doorway.

"Roseann, this is my mom, the Elvis freak," said Julie. "Mom, Roseann."

"Hi Mrs. Jackson," Roseann said, returning the woman's grin.

"Oh, please, call me Sue," she said. The woman had dark brown hair and brown eyes like Julie's, but there the resemblance ended. Julie was taller and bigger boned with short, thick hair. Her mother's hair was thinner and lay in waves almost to the middle of her back, making her look much younger than Roseann suspected she was. Like Julie, she seemed to be someone who didn't know a stranger.

Julie pulled Roseann by the arm. "Come on, I'll show you the rest of the apartment, which should take about three seconds."

She wasn't kidding. An archway led to a small kitchen, and beyond that was the bathroom. The kitchen table was in the corner of the roomy living area. Roseann didn't see any bedrooms.

"Where do you sleep?" she asked Julie.

"The couch pulls out into a bed." Julie pointed at a flowered sofa under the windows. "That's mine. Mom sleeps in there with Elvis," she said, waving towards the sitting room.

"Julie!" her mother admonished, trying to look serious but giggling instead. "Well, I'm heading downstairs." She hooked the long strap of her purse over her shoulder and walked to the doorway.

"Come down later if you want Cokes."

"Mom works in the restaurant next door," Julie explained. "They always give me free drinks."

Roseann nodded. "I like your mom. She seems neat."

"Yeah, she is," Julie agreed.

"My parents are divorced," Julie went on. "My dad was fooling around on my mom and it was a long time before she found out. Before either of us found out. Then, one day, he was gone. None of the bills had been paid and we had to move out of our house into this dump. That was two years ago. Now my mom has to work, which is OK, because before that we were on welfare. Things are a little better now."

Roseann was taken aback. None of her old friends' parents were divorced or had to live in a dingy apartment. The emotions involved were something new to Roseann. She felt both sympathy and admiration for her new friend. Julie was a proud girl, Roseann thought, whose cheerfulness probably covered up many other feelings.

"Do you ever see your dad?"

"Twice a year, at Christmas and my birthday."

Roseann winced. "That's awful."

"I don't want anything from him. Neither does my older brother. He lives in Chicago and hasn't seen Dad since the divorce."

"Well," Roseann said after a long pause, "I know you had a reason to ask me to come here."

"Come on," Julie said, heading toward the door.

22

Julie and Roseann sat in a vinyl-covered booth in Bonnie's Café and watched a fiftyish, overweight woman haul herself onto a stool at the counter. It took the woman three tries to get her body solidly onto the seat. Slamming her purse on the counter, she yelled at the restaurant's owner, Bonnie Cox, to bring her a cup of coffee. The man sitting next to her moved down a couple of stools.

"Come to watch the show, girls?" Sue Jackson set two Cokes in front of them, gave them a wink, and went to tend to another customer.

The woman at the counter laughed loudly, for no apparent reason, as no one was talking to her. She wore pink shorts and a sleeveless top, both of which were stretched tightly over her ample body. She reached into her purse and pulled out a pack of cigarettes, then shouted at Bonnie to bring her some matches.

Roseann looked questioningly at Julie, who leaned over the table and gestured for Roseann to do the same.

"That," she said, "is Sandy Allen's infamous aunt."

Roseann's jaw dropped. She looked back over at the woman, who now had a lighted cigarette dangling from her mouth as she used both hands to pour a ton of sugar into her coffee cup. Part of it spilled on the counter, and she shouted a cuss word loud enough for everyone to hear.

Roseann finally found her tongue. "You're kidding," she said, knowing that, of course, she wasn't.

"A real one-woman spectacle, huh?" Julie commented, taking a sip of her Coke.

The woman was just as awful as Brenda Smart had said.

"No wonder Sandy said what she did," Roseann whispered.

Julie nodded. "Every Friday night she goes on a binge—that's when her boyfriend gets paid and he gives her a wad of money, God knows why. Then she comes in here to sober up. One time she passed out at the counter and Mr. Cox had to take her home. He said she stank to high heaven."

Roseann turned and stared at the woman—she couldn't help it. The image of her being the soft-spoken tall girl's aunt didn't come together. She could see why Sandy didn't want to claim her. Then a sobering thought hit her: Sandy had a lot to deal with, and Roseann knew she couldn't confront her about her lie.

"Thanks for bringing me here," she said to Julie is a subdued tone. "Now I understand things better."

"I thought you might, But it was easier to show you than try to describe it."

Roseann swirled the straw around in her Coke, then looked up at Julie, who was still staring at Violet.

"If Sandy's parents aren't dead, what happened to them?" Roseann asked.

"Well, from what I understand, the mother just dumped Sandy on the grandmother and went back to Chicago, where Sandy was born."

"What about her father?"

Julie shrugged. "No one seems to know anything about him. He sure hasn't offered to come around here."

Violet's loud cackle filled the restaurant just then, causing nearly everyone to turn and look at her.

Sue was standing by the cash register and caught Roseann's eye as she looked up. Sue shook her head and rolled her eyes, then proceeded to ring up a customer's ticket.

A thousand thoughts swirled in Roseann's mind as she headed away from downtown. If what Sandy had to put up with at home was anything like what she had just witnessed, on top of having to deal with her height, the girl must lead a horrible life. And Roseann had seen Sandy routinely use the pay phone after lunch all week. What was that all about?

I won't confront Sandy, Roseann thought, but I need to fine-tune my story before turning it in.

As she walked toward home, Roseann felt lighthearted about her decision. The leaves on the trees along Washington Street, now beginning to turn crimson and yellow, blew softly in the breeze, as if to affirm it.

23

Roseann had been excited about Ashley Stevens' 16th birthday party and sleepover—not only because her best friend was turning 16, but she also would get to see several of her other Indianapolis friends again. Her dad had driven her to the city on Saturday afternoon, and now, Sunday morning, had picked her up after breakfast.

As they drove home, Roseann thought about the overnight trip. Although she enjoyed seeing her friends, Roseann came away disappointed, and she wasn't sure exactly why. They had been happy to see her, of course, and asked about her new school. But once the conversation turned to what was going on at her old school, she felt that she was on the fringes, no longer a member of this tight group of girls that had been together most of their lives. There was one girl at the party whom she didn't even know.

She found out that Kyle was now dating someone else—information doled out cautiously by Ashley, who knew that Roseann had not heard from him since she moved. The other girls talked about teachers she didn't know and events she wasn't a part of. There had been cheerleading tryouts and her former neighbor, Pam, had made the varsity squad along with Ashley. And a new club had formed at school for kids who enjoyed board games, like backgammon and Chinese checkers. Roseann would have liked that.

In the three months that she had been gone, her friends had obviously moved on.

She didn't dare tell them about Sandy Allen—she felt they wouldn't understand why she was so interested in the big girl who was

84

a misfit at Shelbyville High. During the party, Roseann found her mind wandering back to Sandy and her unfortunate circumstances, and to Julie Jackson, an unpretentious and welcome bright spot in her new life. Was she starting to move on, too?

On the way home, Jack Bellamy let Roseann drive the rest of the way after they left Indianapolis. She had obtained her learner's permit during the summer and enjoyed the easy drive down I-74 toward Shelbyville. Her dad asked about the party and she said it was OK. Then she found herself telling him all about Sandy Allen and her story for the *Courier*, and the problems she had encountered.

"Sounds like an interesting girl," her dad mused. "I'd like to see your story when you're done with it."

Roseann was pleased. Since he started his new job, she hadn't seen much of her dad or had any long conversations with him.

"How tall did you say she was?" her dad asked.

"Over seven feet. She thinks she's around seven-foot-three."

"Wow. I wonder when she was last measured."

Roseann glanced at her dad, a pleasant-looking man of medium height whose red hair and gray eyes matched hers. The red hair on his arm, resting on the open car window, shone in the sun. Her dad wasn't embarrassed by the color like she was. It seemed to her almost as if red hair was a bad mark in some people's eyes. She had read that during the Middle Ages women with red hair were often suspected of witchcraft!

"Well," her dad said, "I have an idea. Why don't you invite Sandy over to the house sometime? Maybe for dinner."

Roseann was taken aback. She hadn't thought about doing anything like that. Sandy was just an acquaintance.

"I'll think about it," she said finally.

Roseann spent part of Sunday rewriting her article on Sandy, taking out the quote about Sandy's parents being dead but not mentioning the witchy aunt. As with many of her stories, she made several changes after re-reading it, tightening her prose so that, despite its length, it was a quicker read. She was much happier with the rewrite and was glad for the opportunity to make it better. Sandy had been fine with the first draft of the story, and Roseann decided to show the new version to her the next day without telling her what was omitted. She probably won't even notice, Roseann thought.

She thought a lot about Sandy being an outcast at school—and in public—and how that must feel. Roseann remembered her first day at SHS when she felt disconnected and strange. At that moment, Roseann knew how she could enhance her story on Sandy Allen even further. The next question was, should she invite Sandy to her house for dinner?

Roseann plopped her tray onto the tall girl's table in the lunchroom. Sandy looked startled, as she often did when someone besides a teacher spoke to her.

"Hi," Roseann said, "mind if I join you?"

"Be my guest," Sandy replied.

Roseann unwrapped her turkey sandwich on whole wheat and watched as Sandy took the last few bites of hers. She noticed that Sandy was wearing new, more becoming eyeglasses, which prompted a compliment from Roseann. Sandy offered an embarrassed thank-you.

"I've been meaning to ask you," Roseann ventured, "how would you like to come to my house for dinner sometime?"

Roseann didn't look Sandy in the eye, hoping to keep the invitation casual, expecting Sandy to say no.

Sandy hesitated, Roseann filling the awkward silence by taking a spoonful of her chocolate pudding.

"I don't have any way of getting there," Sandy said, indicating that she might be thinking about it.

"My dad can pick you up," Roseann volunteered. "He has a big car," she added, hoping it wouldn't embarrass this long-legged girl.

To her surprise, Sandy let out a chuckle. "Yeah, that would be helpful," she said. "Would it be OK if I bring my little brother?"

"Sure, that would be fun."

A couple of boys at the next table chose that moment to start singing "The Jolly Green Giant" loud enough for Sandy to hear. As usual, she ignored it.

As they got louder, Roseann turned to glare at them.

"You are SO immature," she shouted at them.

"Ignore them," said Sandy, pushing herself up from the table while the boys whistled as she stood. "Maybe they'll dry up and blow away."

"See you later," she added.

And with that, she ambled out of the lunchroom and disappeared down the hallway.

Roseann couldn't believe she just invited a giantess to her house for dinner. She would have to make sure her brother Scott wouldn't freak out. How she was going to do that, she didn't know.

24

Jack Bellamy held the front door open as Sandy Allen ducked her head coming through the entrance into his family's living room, followed by her four-year-old brother.

Roseann had been peeking out the front window to watch for her dad's car to arrive, and was ready for her guest.

"Hi!" she called out. "I'm glad you could come."

"My pleasure," said Sandy, who seemed to be in a jovial mood. "This is my brother, Joey."

Roseann smiled at the little boy. "Hi Joey," she said. He said nothing and disappeared behind Sandy's long leg.

Roseann's mom came into the room to greet Sandy and Joey and seemed to be unfazed by the girl's size. Then her brother Scott bounded in, and Roseann held her breath. He had been told what to expect, but the sight of someone who towered over him that much made his eyes grow as big as dinner plates.

"Wow!" he said, shrinking back a little. "You're really big!"

"Scott!" Roseann was mortified, hoping his reaction wouldn't embarrass Sandy.

"That's OK," said Sandy, "I'm used to it. Come on over here, buddy," she said to Scott, who had inched closer to his mother.

Scott hesitated, then cautiously approached Sandy, who stuck out her hand to shake his. He just looked at it, then put his hand on top of hers. "Wow," he said again.

Sandy let his small hand rest there while he compared the sizes. A flashback of Delores Pullard in the Fairgrounds tent, with her cousins doing the same thing, hit Roseann as she stood there and watched. It was one thing to observe Sandy at school, where most people were used to her, and another to see her in a circumstance where she was meeting someone for the first time. Her parents were being cool, letting Sandy handle the situation, and Roseann followed suit.

Eventually, Scott shook her hand, then started asking a million questions about her size. She answered all of them matter-of-factly, and Roseann remembered Sandy telling her that she often found it easier to talk to kids than adults because their questions were so honest.

Jack interrupted the inquisition long enough to lead Sandy to the most substantial chair in the living room—his leather recliner—and everyone watched as she lowered herself easily into the chair, her long legs stretched out into the room. Joey climbed up into her lap and rested his head on her shoulder, still not saying anything.

The visit seemed to be going well, and Roseann noted that Sandy was much more animated and friendly in this family home than she was at school. It was like she was a whole different person.

After a while, Scott seemed to be satisfied that all of his questions had been answered. Then he turned to Joey.

"Hey, I have some really neat model trains set up in the basement. Want to see them?"

Joey looked up at Sandy, who nodded her approval. "Sure," he said, climbing down from his sister's lap and following Scott to the basement door.

Roseann watched this exchange in shock: Her bratty little brother was being kind to a stranger! This was way out of his usual comfort zone.

Barbara Bellamy excused herself and headed for the kitchen to finish making dinner, leaving Roseann and her dad alone with the giantess in the big brown recliner.

Jack was taking great interest in Sandy and asked her several questions about her medical condition. Then he asked when she had last been measured, and she replied about two years ago at the I.U. Medical Center in Indianapolis. She was seven feet two-and-a-half inches at the time.

"I know I've grown since then," she mused.

Jack asked Sandy if she would like to be measured again.

"Sure," she said. "I'd like to know how tall I am so I can put it on my driver's license. Whenever I get the thing."

Roseann laughed. Sandy looked over at her and chuckled.

"Hey, I'm taking Driver's Ed next semester," she said in her deep voice. "That should be interesting."

Jack excused himself and went to the basement, then returned to the living room with a twelve-foot tape measure from his tool box.

"This should do it," he said to the tall girl. "Are you up for this right now?"

"Sure," Sandy said, pushing herself up from the recliner.

Jack pulled a footstool into the middle of the room and had Sandy stand next to him. Roseann held the tip of the tape measure to the floor as Jack unrolled the tape to just above Sandy's head, then clicked it into place.

"Looks like you're right at seven-feet-four," he said.

"Wow," said Roseann.

"Got any ceiling light bulbs that need changing?" Sandy joked. She wasn't at all surprised about her height—she said she could tell by the way her clothes fit that she had grown. It didn't impress her as much as it distressed her.

A few minutes later, Mrs. Bellamy invited them into the dining room for dinner and asked Roseann to call the boys. Roseann obliged, heading down the stairs to the basement, where Scott and their dad had set up an elaborate HO-scale train village on a huge table, with two trains running through it.

Roseann was startled at what she saw. Scott had pulled a step-stool over to the table for Joey and was showing him how to work the transformer. The little boy was delighted when he pulled the lever and one of the trains disappeared into a tunnel.

"Not too fast," Scott was saying, showing Joey how far back to pull the lever. "Otherwise the train could fly off the track!" Scott made elaborate wrecking noises and Joey laughed.

Roseann couldn't believe this was her little brother she was watching. He was being patient, kind, and funny, and letting another kid play with his trains—which he never did. She wasn't sure what to make of it.

"Time for dinner," she called.

"What are we having?" Scott asked, not turning around.

"Spaghetti."

"OK."

She knew it would be a while before they came to the table. But she didn't care. She was just happy that Sandy Allen had come for dinner, and that she herself was having a good time with her new friend, the seven-foot-four giantess.

Her friends in Indianapolis would never believe it. And that, she thought, was OK.

25

"Whatcha doing?"

Julie Jackson wandered into the newspaper office toward the end of the period. Her dentist appointment had given Roseann the opportunity to have the room all to herself.

"Finishing up a sidebar to my Sandy Allen story," said Roseann, who had spent most of the previous evening scribbling notes about what she was going to write. It was the end of October and she was anxious for her story on Sandy to run in the *Courier*.

Now there would be two stories, maybe side by side. The first one would be the interview, *The Weather Up Here is Fine*. The second one, the sidebar, was something entirely different. Bold, she thought.

She pulled the paper out of the machine and handed it to Julie for her input.

"*It's OK to be Different*." Julie read the suggested title of the sidebar out loud. "Hey, I like that."

Roseann smiled as Julie settled in on the floor to read her copy.

"'Everyone notices when Sandy Allen walks down the hallways of Shelbyville High School,'" Julie read. "'For Sandy, being the tallest person in the school makes her stand out, a difference that is easily noticeable. High school is a time when most kids try to fit in and be like everyone else, but Sandy doesn't have that option.

"'Some of you reading The *Courier* also might have a physical difference from your classmates, or maybe there's something not so obvious that makes you feel set apart from other kids, like a religious belief or a family situation.

"'This is my first year at SHS, and I feel different because I'm the new girl in school, and a new resident of Shelbyville. And even though I'm making friends and have a job on the newspaper staff, I still feel strange at my new school and miss my old one in Indianapolis. But anyone looking at me wouldn't know I feel that way.

"'Is there something YOU feel different about? Would you be willing to share your feelings with this newspaper's readers? If so, please write them down and put them in the drop box outside the newspaper office on the second floor. Please sign your name if you feel comfortable doing so and include your homeroom number. If you prefer to be anonymous, that's OK too.—Roseann Bellamy, *Courier* staff writer'"

"Wow," said Julie, looking up from the paper. "What a cool idea!"

"Think so?" Roseann was pleased at her friend-and-editor's reaction. "Think it'll fly with Mrs. Musgrave?"

"It's worth a shot. Certainly nothing we've ever done before. When they read about Sandy, and then consider this question, it should make a lot of kids think about their own problems instead of someone else's."

Roseann grinned. "Thank you!"

"No big wazoo," Julie grinned back.

At the end of the period, Roseann turned in her Sandy Allen story and sidebar to Mrs. Musgrave, who promised to look them over and get back with her by the end of the week. With a light heart, Roseann headed toward the cafeteria, hoping to have lunch with Julie and her two pals, Sarah and Mary Anne, whom she was growing fond of. Sarah shared Roseann's love of books and they had already borrowed a few from each other. And she got a kick out of Mary Anne, who was always reading movie magazines during lunch while trying to keep up with the conversation.

It's funny, she thought, how just a few weeks ago she didn't even want to be in the SHS building, and now she was actually looking forward to being with her new friends.

On the way, she decided to stop at her locker, which was located on the first floor near the school office. As she rounded the corner, she nearly ran into Sandy Allen, who was using one of the pay phones, this time before lunch. Sandy didn't see her, but Roseann overheard part of the conversation.

"She did what? OK, I know you can't talk. Don't worry, Sissy will take care of it when she gets home." Sandy sounded distressed and angry. Maybe Violet was causing problems, Roseann thought as she hurried by.

Her mood was more somber when she put her lunch tray down at the girls' table, but everyone greeted her cheerfully. She joined in their conversation—something about an upcoming pep rally—but kept an eye on the cafeteria door for Sandy. She showed up just long enough to buy two apples and disappear back down the hall.

26

Sandy got off the school bus and headed toward her small yellow house with her eyes ablaze. Joey came flying out the front door and grabbed onto her leg, almost causing her to fall. "What happened this time?" she asked her little brother.

"She took a big knife and cut up all my bears. All of them," he told her with a sob catching in his throat.

"That witch," Sandy mumbled under her breath. She could hear Violet in the house, screaming for Joey, then watched her come running out of the house. Their aunt stopped dead in her tracks when she saw Sandy.

"Oh. You're home," she spat out.

"What's the matter with you?" Sandy shouted at her while Joey ducked behind his sister.

"What's the matter with HIM," Violet countered, pointing at the little boy.

"I didn't do it!" Joey said with a sniffle.

"Do what?" Sandy asked him, knowing it was going to be something ridiculous.

"Donny and Ronny were over and they spilled a drink on the floor. Auntie slipped on it and blamed me. So she cut up my toys."

By this time, the neighbors across the street—where Joey's two friends lived—were on their front porch, watching the argument. Sandy looked over and saw them shaking their heads—they had seen this happen many times before.

Violet glared at Joey, then stomped back toward the house.

"If you do one more thing to him, I'll knock you into the next county!" Sandy shouted after her.

"Yeah, yeah," Vi mumbled as she slammed the screen door shut.

Sandy turned to her brother, who was shaking but not crying. He always felt better when Sandy was around.

"One of these days," she promised him, "I'm going to get you and Granny out of here."

Joey nodded, then looked up at her. "Apple, sissy?"

"Yep," she said. "Two this time."

Entering the house, she looked around the living room at the mess Violet had made by cutting the stuffed animals apart. Dora had always kept the house fairly neat, but ever since Violet arrived there were fast food wrappers and beer bottles everywhere. Her aunt not only was an ad for "before" diet pills, she was also a supreme slob.

Out of the three aunts they had, why did they get stuck with the nutty one? she grumbled to herself. Some day, she thought, things will change.

27

Roseann shoved a white paper bag across the dining room table toward Sandy, who had just beaten her at backgammon five games in a row. Ever since they discovered their mutual love for the board game, Roseann had invited Sandy and Joey over more than once to play. Roseann rarely won, and when she did, she felt Sandy had thrown the game on purpose.

The red-haired girl also had discovered that, when Sandy was away from the public eye and her family, she had a great sense of humor and interacted much more easily with others. Sometimes she was downright chatty.

"What's this? My prize for beating you?" Sandy's long fingers reached for the bag, which was bulky and rolled shut at the top.

"Very funny," Roseann said to her friend, who had to sit sideways at the table because her long legs wouldn't fit underneath. "Actually, it's something for you to wear next week when my stories about you come out in the *Courier*. Go on, open it."

Sandy looked puzzled as she reached into the bag and pulled out an oversized black T-shirt. She chuckled as she unfolded it and saw the words I'M WITH SHORTY on the front, with a down arrow extending from the Y.

Sandy stared at it for a while, a big grin on her face. "Where did you get this?"

Roseann grinned back. "I had my dad take me to the Shirt Shack at the mall in Indianapolis. They put custom lettering on T-shirts. They had all kinds of sizes, some even bigger than this, but I thought a 3X would work."

Sandy held the shirt up in front of her blouse, one that Dora had made for her. "It's perfect," she said. "But I don't have any way to pay you for it."

Roseann waved a dismissive hand at Sandy. "It's a gift."

Sandy looked embarrassed. It must have been a long time since she had gotten a gift from a friend. "What a great surprise!" she said.

"Now," said Roseann, "here's what I want you to do. On the day the story and the sidebar are in the paper, I want you to wear this shirt. People are going to be looking at you—even more than they do now," she added, "and this will be a fun distraction. This way, YOU get the first laugh about your size.

"I think it will make you more human—showing people your sense of humor—and more approachable. If I'm wrong, I guess you haven't lost anything."

Roseann watched as Sandy rubbed her fingers across the fuzzy white letters. "It's worth a try," Sandy said, marveling at having a top that came off the rack instead of from Granny's sewing machine or a Lane Bryant catalog.

The two girls listened as shrieks of laughter came from the basement, where Scott and Joey were playing. Roseann's outgoing little brother had become quite taken with Sandy's shy little brother, and the two got along well despite the five-year age difference.

"Sounds like they're having fun," Roseann observed, resetting the backgammon discs on the board for another challenge.

"Yeah." Sandy's voice was deep and her mood turned somber. "He doesn't have much fun at home."

Roseann didn't know where to take this conversation. She was aware that Sandy's crazy aunt made things unpleasant for her family. That was an understatement, so people said, but she knew few details.

"That's too bad," Roseann said to the tall girl.

Sandy nodded. "Violet is a . . . never mind." She looked down at the table.

Roseann put the backgammon dice in the cup and set it on the board. "That's OK. I know about your aunt," she said.

"You do?" Sandy looked up at Roseann.

"Yeah. You must have a lot to deal with."

Sandy's face tightened. "You don't know the half of it," she mumbled, rolling and unrolling the top of the Shirt Shack bag.

Roseann shot a sympathetic look at her friend, not wanting to have an awkward conversation after such a good day. But Sandy was in the mood to talk, and launched into story after story about Violet, how she picked on Joey, and how Sandy refused to acknowledge the fact that Violet had any authority over them or that she was even in the home.

"That's why I take Joey with me wherever I go," she explained. "Every day after lunch I call home to make sure he's OK. It drives me crazy being away from him and worrying about what she's doing. Sometimes he can't talk because she's standing right there by the phone, but I always know when something's wrong."

"Wow." Despite the change in mood, Roseann was pleased that Sandy confided in her. "I guess that's all you can do. But you can bring him over here any time."

"Thanks." Sandy picked up the cup—which disappeared in her large hand—and swirled the dice around in it.

"You ready for another game?" Roseann asked brightly, trying to pull Sandy out of her mood. "I'm gonna beat you this time."

"In your dreams, Shorty!"

28

Roseann woke up early on November 2nd, the day her stories about Sandy Allen were to appear in the *Courier.* She had looked forward to this day with anticipation, especially after the praise she received from her story on Brenda Smart in the last issue. Even though her interview with Sandy had come first, the story on Brenda had to run earlier to coincide with the opening of *My Fair Lady,* in which Brenda had the starring role. Brenda had stopped her in the hallway to thank her, and Mrs. Musgrave complimented her in class, even though that kind of comment embarrassed her.

Of course, it was easy to write about someone who was well-known in school because of her talent. And the photos taken during rehearsal turned out great. But an article about the school misfit and the photo of her towering above Mrs. Sherman in the library could either turn people off, or they could find it revealing because no one knew Sandy well as a person. Roseann hoped it would have a positive effect, even if it just kept the teasing down.

No matter how the story is perceived, Roseann thought, she was glad of one thing: She was able to call Sandy Allen her friend.

Roseann took her time getting ready for school, making sure the little bit of makeup she wore looked right and putting on her favorite yellow sweater. She hoped that Sandy wouldn't chicken out about wearing her I'M WITH SHORTY shirt.

She needn't have worried: When she popped into the library before first period, Sandy was hanging a poster high on the wall, wearing the T-shirt with a pair of black pants.

"You look great!" Roseann told her.

"Thanks. My granny made me these slacks . . . she thought it would go nice with the shirt. I've already gotten a few stares, but I'm used to that."

"The papers will be distributed after first period. I hope everything will be OK."

"I'm not worried." Sandy's deep voice used to startle Roseann, but now she was used to it.

"OK, see you in gym."

By lunchtime, many of the kids were carrying the *Courier* around with their books. Roseann headed toward the cafeteria hoping to see Sandy. She was delighted to find that Julie, Sarah, and Mary Anne had pushed another table next to Sandy's and were ready for Roseann to join them. Sandy had already been through the lunch line and looked startled at the attention.

Julie was grinning and waving a carton of milk in the air. "Come on, Bellamy, hurry up and get your grub so you can eat with us short people!"

As Roseann sat down with her lunch tray, Mary Anne was telling Sandy how cool she thought her shirt was and said how much she liked the article. Sandy looked self-conscious and just said "thank you" to the girl, who had never spoken to her before. She seemed relieved that Roseann had joined the group.

"Hey," Roseann greeted her. "How's it going?"

"OK."

Julie, who had gone all through grade school and junior high with Sandy, told her that the shirt "cracked her up."

"Thanks." Sandy stole a glance at Roseann, who gave her a knowing smile.

A pudgy boy in a gray sweatshirt walked behind Sandy, purposely bumping her on the shoulder with his lunch tray. "Hey freak!" he whispered loudly, then chuckled and walked away.

Roseann nearly came out of her chair.

"Don't," Sandy said. "He isn't worth it."

Mary Anne and Sarah exchanged looks, then regarded Sandy curiously. "How can you put up with that crap?" Sarah said indignantly, her voice raising almost to a squeak.

"After the first 50 times, you get used to it," Sandy said matter-of-factly. "If I let it bother me, I'd be bummed all the time. I don't have time for that."

"Good attitude," said Julie. "But I'd be tempted to tell the creep where he could stick it."

"Me too." Roseann, who had been elated about her article, suddenly felt defeated. She stiffened when another boy came over to their table.

"Hi Sandy. Great story in the paper. Hope you knock 'em dead in basketball this season."

"Thanks."

The boy smiled at her and kept walking.

Roseann looked over at Julie, who was regarding her with amusement.

Well, she thought, this certainly is going to be a day of ups and downs.

The rest of the day, Roseann noticed a lot of kids in her classes were reading the *Courier*. A couple of them who knew Roseann wrote for the paper complimented her on the articles but didn't say anything about Sandy. That's OK, Roseann thought, at least they're reading it. But she truly did wonder how they would react to the "differences" sidebar.

By her last period English class, Roseann was anxious to see how Sandy's day had gone. When Sandy entered the room just after the bell rang, several kids giggled when they saw her I'M WITH SHORTY shirt. Expressionless, Sandy plopped her books down on the desk across from Roseann and maneuvered into the small seat, crossing her gangly legs in the aisle.

Roseann leaned over toward her tall friend.

"How's it going?" she whispered.

Sandy gave her a wide smile, showing those spaces developing between her teeth.

"Not bad. People have been friendlier today and I've gotten a lot of laughs from the shirt."

"Well," said Roseann, "I guess that's something."

"Yep."

Sandy offered her a high-five, and Roseann had to reach way up to get it.

29

Basketball practice wasn't going well for Sandy Allen a few days later. Her left leg—the one where she had had two surgeries to fix the bones that were growing faster on one side of her knee—was starting to bother her more. Her leg still wasn't completely straight, and it was becoming harder to run down the court. She could tell that Coach Murray, although sympathetic to Sandy's physical issues, was getting impatient with her. The tall center was still a good shooter and rebounder as long as she stayed near the basket, but hot pain shot through both knees when she ran. The arches in her feet were breaking down, also, which added to her discomfort.

During the break, Sandy limped over to the bleachers and grabbed a towel. She was sweating as she sat in the second row with her long legs reaching to the floor. After wiping her face, she reached down and rubbed the side of her knee, not that it did any good.

It had not been a good morning at home, either. Violet, who normally slept late, was up at dawn, banging things around in the kitchen. She had yelled at Joey, who had gotten up to see what all the noise was about, so he crawled into bed with Sandy and Granny Dora. When Violet had a hangover, everything Joey did seemed to irritate her. Sandy knew the only reason she kept him was to get the welfare money. Aunt Vi hated taking care of her niece and nephew in spite of getting a home and money each month.

By the time Sandy left early for basketball practice, Violet was already giving Joey grief while Dora watched in silence. Sandy knew Joey was in for another bad day.

Coach Murray interrupted Sandy's thoughts, taking a seat next to her on the bleachers.

"Leg still bothering you?"

Nancy Murray was tall and lanky, with short salt-and-pepper hair and piercing blue eyes. She was a good gym teacher and a demanding coach. She knew she had to keep her team on top of its game if they expected a winning season.

"Yeah. It seems to be getting worse." Sandy glanced at her coach, then looked away, disappointed in herself.

Coach Murray nodded, twisting the whistle cord that hung around her neck. "Have you talked to your doctor about it?" she asked.

"No. I haven't been able to get a ride to Indianapolis."

"Hmmm." Coach Murray watched as Sandy dabbed at the back of her neck with the towel. "Our first game is a week from Friday. Do you think you can handle it?"

Sandy sighed, running her fingers along the eight-inch surgical scar that ran from above the side of her knee to below it. It was ugly and she hated it.

"I don't know," she finally said, keeping her head down. She didn't want to meet her coach's gaze and see her disappointment.

Coach Murray didn't look disappointed—she looked concerned. She also didn't want to start the season with an injured player who might be pushing herself too hard. She knew Sandy's physical issues were different from those of other kids her age, but she didn't know how to help the unusual young woman, who was a key player on the team.

"Maybe I can arrange for you to get a ride to the doctor." Coach Murray put her hand on Sandy's shoulder. "Or maybe he could prescribe some pain medication over the phone. But you really should have that knee looked at," she said. "I don't think you should play if you have that much pain."

"Probably not."

"Why don't you go ahead and hit the showers. You've probably had enough for today." Coach Murray patted Sandy's shoulder, then stood up and blew her whistle, signaling that the break was over. She turned and gave Sandy a thumbs-up as she headed back to the court and her team.

Sandy got up slowly and tried to keep her leg as straight as she could while heading for the locker room. She liked taking showers at school because she couldn't do that at home, and this time she wouldn't have all the other girls staring at her body.

After getting dressed, Sandy put her shorts and sleeveless shirt —one that Granny made so it would be long enough—into her gym basket, then gathered up her books. She took a deep breath and ducked through the doorway of the locker room, leaving behind what would be her last time on the basketball court at Shelbyville High.

30

A week after her articles on Sandy Allen appeared in the *Courier*, Roseann stopped outside the newspaper office to check the box where kids could drop their comments and suggestions. To her astonishment, there were 19 envelopes in response to her *It's OK to be Different* sidebar.

Excited, Roseann dumped her books on the desk and sat down to read them.

Most of them were short and some had misspellings, but all in all they were well done and exactly the kind of feedback she had hoped for.

The first two tugged at her heart:

"I can understand how Sandy feels because I also have a physical difference that has caused people to stare at me and call me names. I was born with a harelip (also called a cleft palate), a facial deformity caused during development as a fetus. I had surgery soon after birth and have had several since then. I will be facing more in the future.

"When I was younger, I talked with a lisp and was teased all through grade school and junior high. I would walk to the bus stop with my brother and sister, and the neighborhood bullies would chant 'Here comes funny lips!' My brother and I got into a lot of fights because I think he was embarrassed, but also felt he had to stick up for me. In class, I would sit at a desk near the wall or the window so only some of the kids could see my face.

"Things are better now that I'm older, but sometimes the

comments still hurt. I've learned to let things roll off my back and not be the burden it was when I was younger. I hope that Sandy can do the same."

M.R.

"I have the opposite difference from Sandy—I am four-feet-two and a dwarf. Most dwarfs prefer to be called 'little people,' but I'm called a lot more things than that! Shrimpy, Midget, Stubby and even worse. Some guys are always trying to pick me up and throw me around, which I hate. Girls think I'm 'cute,' which I also hate. I've never gone out on a date because I don't want to face rejection.

"Life isn't easy when you're short because you can't reach things and always have to ask people to help you. I can do a lot on my own though, and some day I hope to be able to drive. I love sports but I can't play them, so I have to settle for being the team manager, which is more like a mascot. But better than nothing, I guess.

"Fortunately, I have great parents and they don't treat me any differently than my brother and sister. I don't know what I want to be when I grow up (haha), but I'm thinking about working with underprivileged kids because they feel different too."

Joshua Perry

The next one was from a tall blond girl Roseann recognized as being on the varsity basketball team with Sandy:

"My name is Astrid, and that's what makes me feel different from other kids. All through grade school I was called 'Ass-Turd' and I'd come home from school crying. I was named after both my grandmothers, and I tried going by my middle name for a while, but it didn't work. I decided when I got older I would have my name legally changed.

"Then one day my mother explained the origin of the name. 'Astrid' is Old Norse for 'Divine Beauty.' She also told me that her own mother and my father's mom were proud of the names and that she hoped I would be too. Since then I have discovered several famous people named Astrid, including a Viking queen, two members of the Belgian royal family, a Swedish author, an East German athlete, a Scottish musician and a French artist. So I'm in good company. And now I'm proud of my name, too."

Astrid Laura Graham

Other kids' differences weren't as obvious, but still posed challenges:

"I am the lead guitarist of the band RockinBoyz, which plays at a lot of school functions. I didn't use to feel different until the band took off and people I didn't know all of a sudden were saying hi to me in the hallways. That took some getting used to. My dad said that when you do something that puts you in the public eye, you have to expect others to pay more attention to you and treat you differently. OK, I'm cool with that. I just want to be a good musician and have friends who like me for who I am, not what I am."

Alex Dunkin

"I have the exact same name as one of the Beatles, so I guess that makes me different. Every time I tell someone my name I get a reaction, like, 'Is that your real name?' Sometimes it's a pain but most of the time it's fun. I think it's cool to have the same name as a rock star in one of the world's most famous bands!"

George Harrison

"P.S. I named my dog Ringo!"

"My name is Lynn Whitney and I want to point out that even something positive can make you feel different. I have the highest grade point average in the senior class and could be the Valedictorian at graduation. I've been called 'brain-girl' and other names, but usually in a friendly way. But there's a lot of pressure in being smart because you always feel like you can't fail at anything or you might disappoint your parents and other people. So even though doing well in school is an accomplishment, it still makes me feel different because I'm held to a higher standard than most of my classmates."

Lynn Whitney

"We feel different because we are twins and cheerleaders. People are looking at us all the time, but not like what Sandy experiences. While being popular is nice, we always have to look our best and try to keep our grades up, and sometimes that isn't easy even though it's expected of us. We also feel different because our aunt is the librarian and we don't know anyone else who has an adult relative working in the school. (She even threw us out of the library once for being noisy!)

"It was nice to get to know Sandy better through this article and we hope that a lot of people respond to it. We learned a lot from it because we thought we were just like everyone else, but realized we were different after all."

Hayley and Holly Sherman

"We feel different because we are three of only a few black kids at Shelbyville High," read the next note. "There have been a few incidents of name-calling, mostly when we were in younger grades. Sometimes we are stared at because people expect us to act a certain way because of our race. Then they're surprised to find out we're just like everyone else, only with darker skin."

Justin, Desiree and Marisol

There also were a few anonymous letters.

"On the outside I look like any other high school senior at SHS. On the inside, I feel different because my older brother was killed in Vietnam, and I don't think most teenagers understand how hard it is to lose someone who has been your hero all your life. He's just a different kind of hero now. His death has put a

hole in our family and I don't know how to resolve that. Someday I hope to be able to cope with this a lot better than I am now."
Anonymous

Roseann's mouth dropped open. She knew it was from Randy, her senior editor, who seemed to be so easygoing. Julie had told her about Randy's brother, and she remembered the day of the anti-war rally and how Randy had stood by himself off to the side, just looking on. I wonder if I should say anything to him, she thought.

Another anonymous letter was from a student who was adopted.

"I have always felt different because I am adopted. Not just at school, but everywhere. It's not that I have a bad life, because my parents are great. But I always feel like part of me is missing. Someday I hope to look up my biological parents and get some answers to questions that are bothering me, like why they gave me up.

"I'm not going to sign this because I hope I can speak for other adopted kids in this school who might feel the same way I do. Thanks for the opportunity to bring our differences out into the open."

A few of the other letters also were anonymous, including two from students who said they were gay, one whose dad was in jail and another dealing with divorced parents. Two letters were from former new kids in school—including Allison Tanner, the girl Roseann had met in gym class that first day—who said they had felt the same way Roseann did when they started at SHS.

Roseann looked at each one as if it were a small treasure, a part of someone's heart revealed on paper. These kids had a lot of courage, more than she expected. She also felt guilty for not being totally honest about her own differences in her article: Being the new girl at SHS wasn't the only thing that she felt set her apart from her classmates. She also felt different because of her carrot-colored hair and a misbehaving younger brother who sometimes put her family at odds with each other. She even felt her choice of vocation—a journalist—set her apart from her peers, but she didn't feel bad about that. She didn't see herself being a teacher or a secretary or a nurse like some of her friends. After all, women were starting to find their way into several male-dominated professions, and she was glad of that!

Now she had the task of figuring out how to present these letters in another article. She knew she would have to treat them sensitively and put a positive spin on the fact that these kids revealed personal information in order to help other kids understand them better. She also hoped she could get some of them to agree to have their pictures taken for the *Courier*.

Roseann tucked the letters into a folder. Mrs. Musgrave will be able to help her find the right approach, she thought. And maybe, just maybe, I'll get an "A" in my journalism class this semester!

31

A couple of weeks after Roseann's article on Sandy Allen appeared in the *Courier*, the mostly positive attention Sandy got was starting to die down. Sandy herself was glad: While things were better for her at school, she still felt uncomfortable when the focus was on her. She had bigger things to worry about every time she walked out her front door and left Joey with Aunt Violet.

Thanksgiving was coming up, but it wasn't going to bring the typical joy and family harmony. That didn't exist in the little house on Hamilton Street. Violet would cook a turkey, but it would taste like shoe leather, like all the meat she prepared.

Even the few moments of contentment proved unnerving. The previous Sunday, Sandy had gone to her friend Carole's house for a birthday luncheon. Dora had gone to church and Joey and Violet were asleep when Sandy left.

When she got home, there were two police cars in front of her house. Violet, who was still in her nightgown, was arguing with one of the cops. Dora looked distraught. Joey was across the street on the neighbors' porch and several people along the block were watching the scene.

"What's going on?" Sandy demanded, glaring at Violet, then looking at a policeman, who apparently had taken a baseball bat away from her aunt.

"It seems that this woman—your aunt, isn't it?—was chasing a young child around the neighborhood with this bat. The neighbors called . . . they were afraid he'd get hurt."

Sandy was livid. Her uncle had gone to the Evangelical Methodist Church on the corner to fetch Dora, who tried to calm Violet down. Joey wouldn't come back across the street even with Sandy there.

"Just throw the witch in jail!" Sandy shouted.

"No, please, no," Dora begged. "Just leave her alone, she'll get over it." She was on the verge of tears. After all, this mess of a person was her daughter.

Sandy backed down, although deep inside she didn't want to. But she couldn't stand her granny being upset, and she knew Dora would never press charges.

"You take care of that bat," she said to the officer, "and I'll take care of this one."

Sandy took a step toward Violet, who ran into the house, while the policeman put the baseball bat into his squad car. "Good luck," he said. It wasn't the first time he had dealt with Violet.

Dora apologized to Sandy for leaving the house. "I just want us all to get along," she said tearfully.

"It wasn't your fault," Sandy told her. She went across the street to get Joey, who was still scared to death.

Short of taking him to school with her, Sandy couldn't keep him away from Violet.

Then, in a moment of anger and frustration, Sandy thought about how to resolve the situation.

"You're WHAT?"

Sandy dumped the dice onto the backgammon board and moved several spaces, sending one of Roseann's discs to the center.

It was Saturday night and the girls, along with Scott and Joey, had polished off two large pizzas. The boys were playing in the basement and Sandy and Roseann were on their fourth game of backgammon.

"I am sort of thinking about getting a gun," Sandy repeated, looking down at the board to avoid Roseann's incredulous stare.

"A gun," said Roseann, feeling the words hang heavy in the air.

Sandy had told the baseball bat story to Roseann and said how frustrated she was that Violet got away with so much, even with the police.

"The law doesn't seem to be able to protect us. I figure if I got a gun, it could just accidentally go off and . . . you know . . ."

Roseann stared at Sandy while the tall girl ran a finger along the side of the backgammon board.

"You're serious, aren't you," Roseann said. "And if you are, you're nuts."

Sandy made a gutteral noise in response.

"How would you even get one?" Roseann pressed.

"There's a pawn shop over on Washington Street."

"You can't buy a gun—you're only 16!" Roseann said, thinking that being reasonable was a good route to take in this weird conversation.

"I know."

"OK," Roseann said, "let's say you do this, um, scary thing. What will it accomplish?"

"Ding-dong, the wicked witch is dead!" Sandy sang the words to the *Wizard of Oz* song in her deep voice, waving an invisible bell in the air.

Roseann giggled in spite of herself.

"Look," Sandy said, "I don't have a lot of options. Joey still has a year before he can go to school and get away from her. She'll kill him by then."

"I don't get it," Roseann said. "Why would she want to hurt him? I thought she wanted the welfare money." Lately, Roseann was finding out way more about government assistance than she wanted to know.

"Beats me."

Roseann took a sip of Coke and tried to think what to say next to her friend.

"Well," she mused, "let's say something happens and no one believes it's an accident, or something goes wrong, and you end up getting blamed for it. You get sent to jail and Joey loses his protector. And imagine what that would do to Dora."

Sandy didn't speak for a while, digesting the consequences of what she was contemplating.

"Yeah, you're probably right," she said finally. "It's a big risk. Sounded good to me last Sunday, though."

Roseann rolled the dice and managed to get her disc out of the center, then bring another one from behind to protect it. Just like Sandy and Joey, she thought to herself.

The girls played three more games in relative silence. Roseann actually won two of them.

Before packing up the game, Sandy cleared her throat with a deep rumbling sound. She looked over at Roseann with sadness and resignation in her eyes.

"Thanks," she said to Roseann. "I guess I needed someone to talk some sense into me."

Roseann gave her a slight smile, then started singing "Ding-dong, the wicked witch is dead!"

They both looked at each other and burst out laughing.

The week of Thanksgiving, Roseann put the finishing touches on an *It's OK to be Different* follow-up article. Mrs. Musgrave had decided to accept Roseann's own idea: they needed to print some of the responses. The advisor thought the school paper had an opportunity to analyze the school climate as a result of the Sandy stories. Because of the holiday, Roseann would have only one day of classroom time to finish it before the next *Courier* deadline.

It was a bit complicated. They would need to get permission from the letter-writers, some of whom, she thought, probably would insist on being listed as "anonymous." Some might not want their letters printed at all. But, when she rushed around locating the people who had responded to the sidebar, she was pleased that most of them gave her permission to print their letters and their names. Several agreed to have their photos taken for the follow-up article, which would run a month after the stories on Sandy.

Joshua Perry, the dwarf, was a real ham with a great sense of humor. He wanted to have his photo taken with Sandy, which she agreed to, wearing her I'M WITH SHORTY shirt. The *Courier* photographer shot Astrid Graham, the basketball player who had been unhappy with her unusual name, in action during a game, and rock band leader Alex Dunkin's photo was done as a portrait with his guitar.

Roseann had never done a follow-up article before and felt positive about the challenge—the kids had given her some good quotes and did not seem shy in revealing their feelings about being different. Julie Jackson was going to edit the story, since she had also edited the Sandy Allen package.

But Roseann also was saddened by the fact that Sandy had quit the basketball team because of her bad leg and feet. She hoped this wouldn't mean more surgery or other health problems for Sandy, who already was maxed out on stress. Still, Sandy managed to keep her grades up and seemed almost relieved to not be on the basketball team.

Although the teasing about her size hadn't totally stopped, it certainly had died down quite a bit since Roseann's story in the *Courier*. And Julie, along with Sarah and Mary Anne, often ate lunch with Sandy when she was receptive to having company. She still left the lunchroom early to call home, but the other girls didn't question it and Roseann didn't reveal what she knew about the situation.

Some things, she thought, required you to help preserve a friend's quiet dignity. It was the least she could do.

32

Sandy Allen climbed onto the school bus and sat in the back row, where the seat went all the way across and she could stretch her long legs into the aisle. The Sunshine Society had just visited the local nursing home to cheer up the residents, some of whom had no family to visit them or had been forgotten by relatives.

A couple of the elderly women at the home had been startled by Sandy's size, but she immediately put them at ease by sitting in a chair that took her closer to their level and asking them questions about their lives. Because of her own grandmother, Sandy had great respect for older people.

She liked the organization's outings because they made her feel useful to others and forget her own problems, at least temporarily. It felt good to belong to a group in which she wasn't on the outside looking in. The other kids treated her well, as would be expected from a group dedicated to serving others.

Sandy pulled her yellow Sunshine Society folder out of her stack of schoolbooks and read the creed:

> With love in my heart, forgetting self, and with charity for all, I will make the object of my life helpfulness and kindness to others. I shall try to fit myself to give intelligent service in making my community a safer and more beautiful place in which to live. Thus will my own life become rich and complete.

Mrs. Jeffries, her English teacher, had been right about the group being a good fit for her, Sandy thought. She would be grateful for a life that was rich and complete—and even more grateful for one that was just normal. She felt that she could cope with her size if everything else around her wasn't such a challenge.

Sandy returned the folder to her stack of books and smoothed the skirt on her yellow dress. The group's colors—yellow and white—carried over into what they wore, and Granny had stayed up late the night before to finish sewing the dress. It was just as nice as the store-bought ones the other girls wore, Sandy thought. She loved her granny and everything that Dora did for her.

Her mind jumped back to when she first came to Shelbyville from Chicago, where she was born. She didn't remember it, of course, because she was only a few months old, the product of one of her own mother's casual liaisons with a man whom she wasn't even sure was her real father. A neighbor had told her about it just a couple of years ago, a story that Dora would never have repeated to her.

"Your mama, she came down here all by herself with you in a dresser drawer," the neighbor had said. "She handed you to your granny and said, 'Here, you can have it.' Then she disappeared, and she's been gone ever since."

Dora had done a good job raising her, and things were fine until Violet showed up with Joey three years ago. And she, too, was Dora's daughter. So she got to stay—and take over.

Sandy looked out the window of the bus. It already was dark out and there had been a dusting of snow the night before that still lingered. Back to reality, she thought. Back to life on Hamilton Street.

When she got home, things were quiet in the house. Violet had made dinner and gone off to her room. Dora and Joey were eating off TV trays in Sandy's bedroom and watching television.

Thank God, Sandy thought. She had way too much homework to do to be bothered with any family drama tonight. Dora had told her it was important to get a good education if she wanted to succeed in life, and she intended to do just that. It had been a good day. Sandy wished she could have more of them. Maybe they would even get through the Thanksgiving holiday and the weeks beyond.

33

Christmas break came and went much too quickly for Roseann. A few months ago, she never would have believed that her life in Shelbyville could be so busy.

Sandy and Joey visited a few times during the holidays, and Sandy had brought over a new card game called Uno, which was a lot of fun and could be played by all ages. Even Joey enjoyed it, and Roseann had never heard him laugh so much when he was able to give someone a "draw four" card.

For Christmas, Roseann had given Sandy a new funny T-shirt that she had made at the Shirt Shack. Since people were always asking Sandy how she got so tall, the new shirt, in Sandy's favorite color of blue, said "How'd you get so short?" It was a big hit with Sandy, who had become a little more outgoing since the *Courier* articles about her had appeared and was willing to joke more about her size.

Sandy's gift to Roseann was a box of scenic Indiana note cards created by a local photographer, along with a sheet of stamps and a new pen. She knew Roseann liked to keep in touch with her friends in Indianapolis and a pen pal who lived in Alaska. "This is perfect!" Roseann had told her friend.

The boys had gotten each other candy, which was gone before the day was over.

Roseann also had spent time with Julie Jackson and helped her put up a holiday display in the local museum that housed Shelbyville history. And Randy Kozlowski had asked her on a movie date, which she enjoyed, although she thought Randy could sometimes be a little more intense than the boys she knew in Indianapolis. But Randy treated her well and she liked his company. Maybe his intensity was connected to his brother's death.

Roseann's brother Scott had put a damper on her parents' plans for New Year's Eve by having a temper tantrum over something trivial. Roseann was supposed to babysit him while their parents went out with friends, but at the last minute they had to cancel. It was too late for Roseann to make her own plans so she stayed home and read a book, which she actually enjoyed. She had finally gotten her Shelbyville Library card and brought home several teen novels to read.

She also spent time working on her next *Courier* story, an interview with one of the history teachers who had spent the previous summer backpacking in Europe. It was an interesting story full of unusual adventures in the catacombs of Rome and the Isle of Capri, and Roseann was happy Mrs. Musgrave had chosen her for the assignment.

Roseann thought she might get to go to Indianapolis for a couple of days to visit Ashley, but she just ran out of time.

Surprisingly, she wasn't that disappointed.

The day after Christmas vacation, Sandy Allen came to school wearing her new T-shirt and shorter hair that came to just below her ears. With her newer glasses, Roseann thought she looked much better than she had at the beginning of the school year. Sandy would never be a pretty girl, but she made the best of what she had, including a better attitude toward herself.

Roseann's *It's OK to be Different* follow-up story had come out in the *Courier* at the beginning of December, and she was still getting positive comments about it a month later. She had heard from most of the kids who were featured in the story, who thanked her for doing it.

"I feel like I've been relieved of a big secret," one had said.

"People are treating me better," said another. "I showed the story to my parents and they had no idea I felt that way."

Joshua Perry, the small boy with the big sense of humor, had become a minor celebrity because of the story. "I'm going to be in the school talent show!" he told Roseann in a note that he dropped off at the newspaper office. "I'll be doing comedy about being so short. Please come!"

Roseann couldn't have been more pleased. The greatest tribute to her writing, she thought, was knowing it had an impact on readers and that it could make a difference in someone's life. The kids' treatment of Sandy had improved, and although the teasing and staring would probably never stop altogether, at least it had slowed down. But it wasn't just the stories in the *Courier*: Sandy's ability to ignore her detractors made it less fun for them.

The one thing Sandy couldn't ignore, Roseann knew, was her home life. It was far more troubling to Sandy than her oversized body.

34

With semester finals coming up, Sandy got on the school bus with a pile of books. Her first day back to school after Christmas break was busy with reviewing past material in all of her classes. She always dreaded the tests but usually did well on them. Without much of a social life, she could concentrate more on school work. That is, when Violet wasn't acting out.

When Sandy had called Joey at noon that day, he seemed to be distracted on the phone and couldn't tell her what was going on. He didn't seem to be hurt, but Sandy knew that when she got home, she'd be facing something that Vi had done during the day.

A neighbor from across the street approached Sandy as she got off the bus on the corner.

"Your brother is fine," she said without any preliminary greeting. "He spent the afternoon at my house playing with Donny. Your aunt was a little tipsy and went into the drugstore. They threw her out but she kept coming back in, so they called the cops. She spent most of the afternoon at the police station, and they finally let her go so she walked home."

The drugstore was only a couple of blocks from Sandy's house. Violet liked to hang out there because it was a close place to buy cigarettes. Sandy frequently took Joey there for a candy treat.

"Thanks," Sandy told the neighbor. "I wish they had kept her."

The neighbor nodded. She was all too familiar with the goings-on at 105 South Hamilton Street.

Sandy approached the back parking lot of Shelbyville High with anticipation. After several days of Driver's Education class work and learning the rules of the road, today was the first day her group was actually going to get behind the wheel of a car.

The second semester of her junior year held a lot of promise for Sandy. Because of her bad leg, she dropped out of gym class and took a study hall, which gave her more time to do her homework. She also had gotten notice that she would be inducted into the National Honor Society for her academic achievements. Granny was so proud!

And now, she was going to learn how to drive. Sandy had watched her uncle and others who had driven the family around and felt she could handle a car. She planned to get a job during the summer and save money for a vehicle so she wouldn't have to walk everywhere.

The instructor unlocked the door of a mid-size, four-door sedan for Sandy and two boys in her class.

"Ladies first," he said, holding the driver's-side door open.

Sandy eagerly ducked her head inside the car and saw that the steering wheel was too close to the seat for her large frame.

"Can you move the seat back, please?"

The instructor got in and moved the seat back as far as it would go to accommodate Sandy's long legs.

"Thanks." Sandy ducked back into the car and, leading with her right leg, tried to slide behind the wheel. It was too tight a fit, and she struggled to get back out.

The two boys turned away from her and snickered.

"Try taking your coat off," the instructor suggested.

Sandy had on a heavy winter coat that she had ordered out of a men's catalog. Starting to feel anxious, she unbuttoned the coat and handed it to the instructor. I've got to fit into this car! she told herself.

Sandy tried once more to get behind the wheel, sliding in backwards and then bringing her legs around to the front. The boys and the instructor watched intently as she tried to make her long legs fit under the steering wheel. Finally, she got them under the wheel, but she couldn't stretch them out.

She sat there for a minute with tears stinging her eyes. It wasn't going to work and she knew it. Her hopes of driving were dashed right there in the Shelbyville High parking lot.

Finally, she sighed and maneuvered her way out of the car.

"Is this the only car available? Is there a full-sized car we can use?" she asked the instructor.

"No," he said, "This is all they gave us. I'm sorry."

"OK," she said. "I guess this isn't going to work for me."

"I'm sorry," the instructor said again. "Maybe you can take private lessons in a larger car."

"Yeah. Maybe."

Sandy put her coat back on and picked up her purse. She glanced at the boys, who now were regarding her with sympathy.

"Sorry Sandy," one said.

"What a bummer," the other one offered.

Sandy nodded, not wanting to talk to anyone, and turned to go back into the building. Halfway there, she reached into her coat pocket and pulled out a handkerchief to wipe away the tears that were streaming down her face.

35

During spring break, Roseann and her dad accompanied Sandy to her doctor's office for a checkup and to have her height measured.

Jack Bellamy pulled up in front of the yellow house on Hamilton Street and honked the horn. Roseann had never been invited inside Sandy's house, so she waited in the back seat for her friend and little Joey to come out. There was enough room in the front seat for Sandy to sit facing forward in the big Buick, with her legs pulled up practically to her chin.

Joey scrambled into the back seat with Roseann, clutching a couple of toy cars. After several visits to the Bellamys' house, he had grown comfortable with Roseann's family and wasn't as shy as he used to be. Going anywhere with his sister was an adventure for him, so he offered an enthusiastic "Hi" in his husky, little-boy voice.

Dr. Bennett's office was located not far from Shelbyville Hospital. The nurse greeted Sandy warmly and ushered everyone into the doctor's office; then Dr. Bennett came in and asked Sandy to take off her hi-top tennis shoes and stand against the wall.

"Do you think I've grown any?" Sandy wondered, towering over the doctor, who was at least six feet tall.

"We'll see," he said. Since the regular scale and height machine only went to seven feet, he brought out a 12-foot tape measure and placed a chair next to where Sandy was standing. He had the nurse hold the bottom of the tape measure while he climbed up onto the chair to get an accurate height.

"How tall do you think you are?" he asked, making a mark on the wall at the top of Sandy's head.

"At least seven-five" she replied in her deep voice, rolling her eyes toward the ceiling.

Dr. Bennett asked Sandy to step away from the wall while he aligned the tape measure with the mark he had made.

"You're now seven-feet-five-and-5/16ths inches," he declared. "I'd say you've grown a bit."

"Wow," Roseann and Joey exclaimed together. Jack Bellamy looked impressed.

Sandy wasn't sure how she felt about such a revelation. Just a few months ago Mr. Bellamy had measured her at seven-feet-four. The more she grew, the more she outgrew her clothes and the more health problems she encountered. She told Dr. Bennett about quitting the basketball team and asked what other things could happen in the future.

"Well—is it OK if I speak in front of your friends?" Dr. Bennett said. "I can talk to you about the acromegaly and how that will affect your growth, but you'll have to see your surgeon for any questions about your leg. Gigantism, as you know, can affect you internally as well, especially your eyesight."

Sandy nodded. Her prescription had changed quite a bit when she got her new glasses in the fall. "So what can I do?"

Dr. Bennett cleared his throat and looked squarely at his patient, who had taken a seat in the exam room with Joey on her lap.

"Well, as you know, your growth is probably caused by a tumor on your pituitary gland. At some point, you'll stop growing taller, but your extremities and internal organs will be affected by the excess growth hormone. You might want to think about seeing a specialist in Indianapolis, and if it's a tumor, get it removed before your problems get worse."

Roseann sucked in her breath. Sandy had mentioned this during their interview and knew her family was not in favor of the brain surgery it would require.

Sandy sat expressionless. It wasn't a surprise to her.

"I'll look into it," she said with resignation.

"Good," said Dr. Bennett. "I'll make some calls and put you in touch with the best surgeon at the medical center."

Jack Bellamy assured Sandy that he would take care of any transportation she needed to the hospital. "Thanks," she said, looking at the floor.

"Are you gonna get your head cut open Sissy?" Joey looked upset.

"Probably. And all my brains are gonna fall out," she told him, sounding more light-hearted than she surely felt.

"Cool," he said, running one of his little cars up his sister's long arm.

36

The next morning, Roseann sat bolt upright in bed. Sandy was seven-feet-five-and-5/16ths inches tall!

She jumped out of bed and went to her file cabinet, pulling out the obit for Delores Pullard, which she had read dozens of times. "Delores Ann Pullard Johnson, believed to be the world's tallest woman . . . measured seven-feet-five inches at the time of her death."

Roseann's gray eyes grew big and she felt her heart leap. Sandy was taller than Delores! Could she be a world record-holder?

It was 9:30 on a Saturday morning and the library didn't open until 10. Roseann hurriedly brushed her hair and teeth, pulled on a pair of jeans and a sweatshirt, and nearly ran 10 blocks to the Shelbyville library. She arrived just as the door was being unlocked by one of the librarians, who looked startled when Roseann rushed past her and headed for the reference desk.

"I need to see a book about world record-holders," she said breathlessly. The librarian nodded and took Roseann to the section she needed, pulling out a thick hardback titled *The Guinness Book of World Records*. Roseann had never heard of this book. She immediately took it to a table and pulled a note pad and pen out of her pocket.

The very first of its 12 chapters was titled "The Human Being." Roseann flipped through it and came upon a photo of the tallest man who ever lived, Robert Wadlow, who was from Illinois and reached a height of eight feet 11 inches before he died in 1940. The photos of this man were amazing!

Then Roseann found the entry she was looking for: "Tallest Living Woman."

"The tallest living woman is believed to be a eunuchoidal giantess named Tiliya (B. 1947) who lives in the village of Saidpur in Bihar State, northeastern India. She stands seven-feet-five inches tall."

"Holy cow!" Roseann said out loud. Sandy was taller than this woman by 5/16ths of an inch!

The entry also mentioned Delores Pullard Johnson as "the tallest woman recently living" and gave her stature as seven feet five-and-a-half inches, a half-inch taller than the height mentioned in her obit. If that height was accurate, Delores had been 3/16ths of an inch taller than Sandy. But she was gone, and Tiliya was shorter than Sandy, possibly making her friend the world's tallest woman!

Roseann copied down all the information. Because it was a reference book, she couldn't check it out of the library, so she wrote down the contact information for the publishers, Guinness Superlatives Limited, in Middlesex, England. She would have to contact them soon to let them know about Sandy. But first, she had to let Sandy know what she discovered!

Roseann ran all the way home, pumped with excitement over the possibility that Sandy's size, which had always been a problem, could make her famous.

She leaped up the steps of her house and flung open the door.

"Mom! Dad! I have something fantastic to tell you!"

"Get out! No kidding?"

Sandy Allen's deep voice boomed over the phone at Roseann.

"All we have to do now is contact the publisher and see what we have to do to see if you qualify as the world's tallest woman," Roseann said.

"That would really be something," Sandy said quietly, letting the information sink in. "I'll guess I'll have to learn how to stand up straighter."

Roseann's dad thought it would be best to expedite the paperwork that could get Sandy into *The Guinness Book of World Records*. He called the publishers overseas and wrote down what they needed and where to send it. Then he called Dr. Bennett, who agreed to meet with him, Roseann and Sandy at his office the following Monday.

Jack Bellamy brought his camera and took photos of Dr. Bennett measuring Sandy to send to Guinness Superlatives Limited, along with an affidavit listing Sandy's height and the day she was measured. It was signed by Dr. Bennett and witnessed by his office nurse and Roseann's dad.

The next day, the paperwork was mailed to England.

All they had to do now was wait.

37

Three weeks after spring break, Sandy Allen's life changed forever.

"Meet me at Bonnie's Café in an hour. Ask Julie to come too, if you want."

Sandy's voice was mysterious with a hint of excitement. Roseann had just gotten home from school and had started on her homework when Sandy called. She thought it was odd to be meeting downtown so close to dinner time.

Oh well, she thought, it must be important.

Julie Jackson was already seated at a table in the back of the café with a Coke and an order of fries in front of her. When Roseann showed up, Julie's mom, Sue, brought over another Coke. It was her night to work at the café.

A few minutes later, Sandy Allen ducked through the doorway with Joey in tow. She settled into the chair across from Roseann—sitting sideways, as usual—and produced a large envelope from under her jacket, plopping it on the table. A grin was playing at the corners of her mouth.

Roseann pulled an official-looking piece of paper out of the envelope. It read:

"This is to certify that Sandra Elaine Allen, of Shelbyville, Indiana, United States of America, at seven-feet-five and 5/16ths inches, is the World's Tallest Woman. Guinness Superlatives Limited, Middlesex, England."

"Omigod!" Roseann shrieked. "You got it! Omigod!"

"Got what, Sissy?" Joey looked confused.

"Wow, cool!" said Julie, grabbing the certificate away from Roseann. "This is awesome!"

Roseann's heart was pounding—she couldn't believe that just a few weeks ago, she and Sandy had talked about the possibility of Sandy Allen being a world record-holder. Now it was a reality!

The girls' shouting was drawing attention in the café, where people were starting to come in for dinner. Sue came running over to see what the fuss was all about and clapped her hand over her mouth when she read the certificate.

"Congratulations!" she said to Sandy, who at this point was starting to look embarrassed.

By this time, everyone in the café was looking at the girls and Joey, who was working his way through Julie's fries. Roseann looked at Sandy, a shy, private girl who suddenly was feeling some very public emotions. Sandy looked both happy and stricken.

"Go ahead," Sandy said, tapping into what Roseann was thinking. "It's going to be all over the place anyway."

Roseann stood up and faced the room full of people. Julie joined her.

"We are celebrating tonight because our friend, Sandy Allen, has just been certified as the tallest woman in the world by the *Guinness Book of World Records*," she announced. "Please join us in congratulating her."

Sandy listened to the cheers and clapping as she looked down at the table, then looked up and gave everyone a little wave.

Roseann sat down, flushed with excitement. Bonnie Cox appeared with some burgers and fries "on the house" and gave Sandy a thumb's up. Sue Jackson, who was shorter standing up than Sandy sitting down, stood nearby, grinning.

"This," said Julie, "is definitely a big wazoo."

It sure is, Roseann thought. What will this mean for Sandy, a quiet girl who isn't used to the limelight? I guess time will tell, she mused, taking a bite of her cheeseburger.

38

It only took one day for the media to get wind of the new world record-holder in Shelbyville, Indiana.

A reporter and photographer from the local paper, *The Shelbyville News*, were at the high school by mid-morning to interview Sandy and take her picture for the afternoon edition.

"I guess making the announcement in a public restaurant wasn't such a good idea," she mused during lunch.

"No kidding," Roseann said, taking a bite of her tuna sandwich.

Sandy hadn't touched her lunch. "I can't eat. The butterflies in my stomach are playing ping-pong with each other."

Roseann—along with Julie, Mary Anne and Sarah—had descended on Sandy's lunch table right after the reporter left. Word of Sandy's record was spreading around school and she was getting way more attention than she expected.

"This is so cool!" Sarah exclaimed.

"Yeah, you're gonna be a celebrity!" Mary Anne grinned. She loved celebrities and now she had one right at her lunch table!

Sandy groaned. "I don't know if I can deal with this," she admitted.

"Sure you can," said Julie, the most positive thinker in the group. "But you'll need to get an agent, or manager, or something, to take care of all this publicity stuff."

"I don't know anything about that," Sandy sighed.

"That's OK, we'll figure it out." Julie raised her milk carton and the other girls followed suit.

"Here's to the world's tallest woman!" Julie announced, and they all tapped their cartons together while Sandy rolled her eyes.

When Sandy got off the school bus she found Hamilton Street full of people. Some were neighbors, others were curiosity seekers. Several of them had cameras. They all cheered when she got off the bus and, despite her embarrassment, she waved at them before ducking into her house.

Violet had been running up and down the street all day saying "My niece is the tallest woman in the world!"

Sandy cringed when she heard that. She wanted no part of Violet's false praise.

Dora was smiling nervously and kept peeking out the window through the curtains.

"What's going on?" Joey didn't understand all the fuss but was pumped up by it, running in and out of the house.

"Sissy got a world record for being tall, so everyone wants to talk to me," Sandy told him, dumping her schoolbooks on the bed.

"Oh. Did you bring me an apple?"

Jack Bellamy made a few phone calls to business associates and located an entertainment attorney in Indianapolis who gave him the name of a local talent agent, John Kelly. Mr. Kelly called Sandy and arranged to meet with her and advise her about handling the media and signing contracts for personal appearances.

The media? Contracts? Personal appearances? All of it scared Sandy to death.

"Don't worry, it'll be fine," Jack told her. "I'll pick you up and you can meet at our house. I'll sit in with you if you want."

Sandy was relieved—she didn't want any strangers coming to her house. And she was glad Roseann's dad would be there to make sure things were done in her best interests.

John Kelly was a tall, affable man in his mid-40s who immediately put Sandy at ease. He understood her family's financial situation and told her he wouldn't charge her for his services unless she got a "paying gig."

"You mean I can make money for being tall?" Sandy was incredulous.

"Of course. People will want you to make personal appearances, sign autographs, have their picture taken with you, that sort of thing."

"Boy, I don't know . . . " Sandy looked over at Jack, then down at the table.

"She's a bit shy," Jack said. "All of this is pretty overwhelming for her."

"I understand," Mr. Kelly said with a smile. "But this situation will knock the shyness right out of her.

"Sandy," John said, turning to the tall girl, "we'll make sure you only do things that you are comfortable with. If you have any concerns or questions, call me any time."

Sandy was quiet for a long time, running a long finger around a spot on the table. Finally, she looked Mr. Kelly square in the eye.

"OK," she said. "But right now, all I want to do is get my high school diploma."

39

During the next few days, all four TV stations from Indianapolis descended on Shelbyville High School to do stories on the teenage giantess who became a world record-holder overnight. *The Indianapolis Star* and *The Indianapolis News* daily papers sent reporters and photographers to talk to Sandy.

The Associated Press and United Press International wire services picked up the newspaper stories, then sent their own reporters for follow-ups. Pretty soon, Sandy Allen's photo would be seen all around the world.

Although it was exciting to have all the publicity at Shelbyville High, the principal, Frank Baker, made sure each request went through him and didn't disrupt the school too much. He also worked with John Kelly to make sure each interview was OK with Sandy, who was trying to keep up with her classes amidst all the hoopla.

The new "star" was filmed shelving books in the library, which kind of freaked out the librarian, who wasn't used to such noise in her quiet corner of the school. Sandy was photographed getting on and off the school bus, standing next to short kids and the tallest teacher in the school, whom she towered over, and going through the lunch line.

"This is all your fault, you know," Sandy said to Roseann in the cafeteria.

"Yeah, I guess it is," replied the young reporter, smiling.

"I want your autograph," Mary Anne announced, shoving her notebook and a pen toward Sandy.

"Me too," said Sarah.

"Let her eat her lunch," said Julie, shaking her head.

Sandy took a bite of her sandwich, then looked at all four girls at her table.

"You know what's weird?" she asked in her deep voice. "I used to get negative attention because I'm a freak. Now I'm getting positive attention because I'm a freak."

"You're not . . . " Roseann started to protest, but Sandy held up her large hand.

"But you guys," Sandy continued, "you guys were my friends before all this started. I want you to know I really appreciate that."

The school year was drawing to a close and Roseann was looking forward to summer. A week before her 17th birthday in May she got her driver's license, and her dad promised her the use of his car. He enjoyed walking to work in good weather, he assured her.

Roseann had been getting A's in journalism all year, and at the final school assembly she got a certificate for Best Feature Story—the one on Sandy Allen and the follow-up, *It's OK to be Different*. She couldn't have been more pleased if someone had handed her a million dollars!

She was excited about her summer job, working part-time in the dime store downtown, and volunteering as a candy striper at Shelbyville Hospital. It would be busy, but Roseann liked to stay busy.

Sandy did well on her finals and made the honor roll despite all the distractions with the media. She refused to do any personal appearances until school was out, and she mandated they couldn't interfere with her summer job working as a clerk in a bail bondsman's office. She referred all requests for appearances to John Kelly, who was kept plenty busy with them.

Her family had to change their phone number due to all the prank calls they were getting, although Violet enjoyed all the attention and would talk to anyone who called. She bragged about Sandy's world record, which the tall girl hated. At least Vi was leaving Joey alone these days—for that, Sandy was grateful.

Sandy's first appearance was at a fancy new hotel in Indianapolis where she was supposed to cut the ribbon during the opening-day ceremonies. Roseann had never seen so many cameras in her life, and most people seemed to be more interested in Sandy than in the hotel. They also went to a restaurant near Shelbyville where Sandy signed autographs and posed for Polaroid photos with the patrons, getting $5 for each picture.

"Can you believe this?" Sandy said after a particularly lucrative day. "People are paying to stand next to me—they used to run the other direction!

"Well," she added, "if they're going to stare at me, I might as well get paid for it."

John Kelly drove Sandy to all of her appearances in his mini-van, which was quite comfortable for the long-legged girl. Joey went, too, and really got into all the free stuff—including great meals—that Sandy would get along the way.

What really blew Roseann's mind, though, was how Sandy was becoming less shy. She was getting really good at interacting with people and had come up with some funny one-liners about being tall ("I guess I ate too many Wheaties" or "The weather up here is fine"). Sometimes she would wear the T-shirts Roseann had given her, which were always a big hit.

"You wouldn't believe what people ask me on these appearances," Sandy told Roseann on the phone after visiting a shopping mall. "They want to know everything from how do I sit on the toilet to how much do I eat for lunch."

"What do you tell them?" Roseann giggled.

"I tell them that, for lunch, I ate three short people."

"You're not going to believe this!" Sandy's mannish voice sounded so excited it almost went up an octave.

It was the day after Sandy's 17th birthday in June and she was calling Roseann from work.

"What's up?" Roseann was ready for anything these days.

"One of the car dealerships over on Broadway called this afternoon. They want to give me a van. FREE!"

"No way!" Roseann nearly shouted. "What's the catch?"

"No catch. I just have to have their dealership name and phone number on the side of the van. They're also going to paint my name and World's Tallest Woman on the side!"

"Wow, that is too cool! But you don't know how to drive!"

"Believe me, I'll learn," said Sandy. "This will be something I can actually fit in."

A new van! Roseann thought as she hung up the phone. Things certainly were looking up for Sandy Allen.

40

Sandy Allen's new greenish-gold van gleamed as she pulled into the Bellamys' driveway and honked the horn. School was scheduled to start the following week and Sandy wanted to treat everyone to hot dogs and root beer at the local drive-in before the end of summer vacation.

Jack Bellamy had been giving her driving lessons, which she mastered easily. The van's seat had to be set back so far it almost touched the seat behind it, but there was plenty of room for her to maneuver her legs. Joey bounced around in the back from one window to another, ready for a new adventure with his celebrity sister.

Because her name and title were splashed in big letters all over both sides of the van, people often honked and waved at Sandy as she drove around Shelbyville.

"I don't think I'll ever get used to this," she said. No one was humming the "Jolly Green Giant" tune within earshot these days.

It had been quite an eventful summer for the world's tallest woman. She had been on several personal appearances and made a decent amount of money doing them. She had enjoyed her summer job—her boss put her desk on cement blocks to raise it up for her legs—and had saved enough money for car insurance. She also was saying she was planning to hook up the bathtub plumbing in her house. Those sponge baths were a bummer.

The city had erected a new WELCOME TO SHELBYVILLE sign out on State Highway 9 that led into town, with the name of the mayor at the top and another sign below that said "Home of Sandy

Allen, the World's Tallest Woman." Sandy did a doubletake every time she saw it. Roseann thought it was awfully cool.

In July, a Guinness photographer came to her house to get a photo for the next edition of the record book, which would come out in October. He shot her standing next to several small children who were looking up at her, as well as with Joey and her granny. The whole neighborhood was excited and came out to watch.

Sandy looked forward to her senior year at Shelbyville High and hoped all the attention about her world record would die down. After all, she had to get an education and plan for her future, probably working in an office somewhere. Anything seemed possible now.

On a beautiful September day, Sandy, Roseann and Julie sat on a bench in front of Shelbyville High School, comparing their class schedules, picked up earlier from the office. Julie groaned when she saw who she had for government—the hardest teacher in the whole school—but was happy that all three girls had landed in same English Composition class, again with Mrs. Jeffries. And, of course, Roseann and Julie ended up in journalism together. Julie was named Senior Editor of the *Courier* after Randy Kozlowski graduated.

Sandy had been nursing a headache all morning and Roseann handed her three aspirin. The new Shelbyville celebrity had felt achy the last few days, and Roseann wondered if it had to do with the acromegaly. She wanted to ask Sandy if she had thought any more about having the brain surgery that would remove the tumor, but decided not to bring it up. If Sandy decides to have the surgery, she'll tell me, Roseann thought.

Just then a couple of girls came out of the building carrying their class schedules. One of them was wearing a denim mini-skirt that showed off her tanned legs. The other had on shorts and a Golden Bears T-shirt. They looked over at the trio on the bench and started pointing at Sandy.

"Hey, look! It's the world's tallest freak and her freak-buddies!"

the tan girl said.

"Yeah! I bet SHE won't get a date for the senior prom!"

Roseann felt anger rise from the pit of her stomach.

"Jealous?" she countered.

"Jealous of what? *That*?" The girl pointed to Sandy, who had her hand on her forehead and was looking down at her lap.

"Get lost," said Julie, trying to stay even-tempered, although it was hard.

"Oh! Look at the little freak-buddies standing up for their giant friend!"

Before they could respond, Sandy took her hand down, slowly stood up and put her hands on her hips.

"Would you care to come over here and say that?" she challenged. Roseann and Julie exchanged glances, wondering where this was going. Sandy usually ignored such things.

"No thanks," said one of the tormentors. "We don't want to get too close."

"Oh, come on," said Julie, jumping in. "It's OK, we've had all our shots."

The two girls just looked at each other, then started to walk away.

"Just don't think you're too great for this school," one of them said over her shoulder. "You think you're a celebrity, but you're still a freak."

"I'm just minding my own business," Sandy shouted after them, her deep voice following the girls down the sidewalk. "I suggest you do the same."

The girls got in their car and drove away while Julie and Roseann turned to look up at Sandy, who had a smirk on her face.

"Low five," said Julie, smacking Sandy's palm with her own.

Here we go again, Roseann thought. Another year of snide remarks. But Sandy handled it well. There was a lot to learn from her oversized classmate.

41

Sandy Allen was now entering her senior year at Shelbyville High with great anticipation. During the summer she had learned how to drive (even though she still took the bus to school), had gained office experience, made some money, learned how to be more eloquent in public and hired an agent to take care of her personal appearances.

She had read about other record-holders and their lives, some of whom elicited her sympathy. Roseann had shared an obituary with her, that of former world's tallest woman Delores Pullard, and learned about her life on the road. That wasn't for Sandy. Not at all.

"No circuses. No sideshows. No carnivals," she said to John Kelly after receiving several offers to tour. "I'm going to high school. That's it."

Things had settled down a bit after the semester started. Then the new edition of *The Guinness Book of World Records* came out in October and she was bombarded with interview and appearance requests all over again. She let John handle it all.

One thing she did agree to was an appearance at a shoe company in Vincennes, Indiana, which offered to give her custom-made shoes in exchange for promoting their store. Sandy readily agreed: Her feet were so cramped in the men's shoes she bought, and it was uncomfortable to walk very far. The company made her a pair of oxfords for every day and a pair of sandals for more formal wear—size 22. She was in seventh heaven!

Sandy also was excited about an opportunity to work in an office again. Shelbyville High, in co-operation with Blue River Vocational

School, offered seniors the chance to work in an office setting a few times a week during school to get experience. Sandy's job was with a local oil company, and she looked forward to each day at her raised-up desk. Her grade would be based on her evaluation by the company.

Just before Christmas break, she and Roseann were at lunch in the cafeteria. She hadn't been harassed for a while, but on this day a few of the freshman boys, who had never seen her before that year, started chanting the "Jolly Green Giant" tune. Roseann was furious, as usual.

Before her red-haired friend's temper got the best of her, Sandy leaned over conspiratorially.

"I want you to do me a favor," she said.

"Sure," Roseann replied. "What?"

"I want you to get me a green shirt and have Jolly Green Giant printed on the front."

"What?" Roseann couldn't believe her ears.

"Remember what you said about getting the first laugh about my size? That should do it."

Roseann thought it over. Of course it would!

"Done," she said.

At the beginning of the second semester, a secretaries group Sandy belonged to announced it would have its annual convention in Albuquerque, New Mexico, that year. Sandy was voted to represent her group, which to Sandy was both exciting and scary. She had never flown before, and how could she leave Joey? Even though he was in kindergarten now, she still didn't trust Violet to be around him.

It was Dora who won in the end. She convinced Sandy that it was a great honor to represent her group and that she needed experiences away from Shelbyville. After much cajoling, Sandy agreed to go, so off she went to experience New Mexico.

"You wouldn't believe how beautiful the mountains are!" she told Roseann by phone after she landed.

"Have a good time," Roseann replied. "I'll check up on Joey."

The school year had flown by, and things went well for Sandy until April, when her headaches started to come more frequently and lasted longer. Her clothes were fitting her more tightly and her forehead looked like it was protruding more. Even her nose was getting broader. It was hard for her to concentrate on school and her work at the oil company.

"I think I'm growing again," she said to Roseann during their weekly backgammon game.

"Oh no. What are you going to do?"

Sandy grew silent. She looked down at the table, which was always her habit to avoid tough situations.

"I guess I should look into having the surgery," she said finally.

Roseann was alarmed but also relieved. They both knew it was inevitable.

"Yeah, you probably should. You don't want to be sick now. You have your whole life ahead of you."

"I know," Sandy replied. "I'm just scared."

"It's OK. We'll all be there for you."

The following week, Jack Bellamy drove Sandy, Joey, Dora and Roseann to see the surgeon in Indianapolis, the one Dr. Bennett had recommended. They went in Jack's car because Sandy didn't want to draw attention to herself, and she noticed she was having more trouble fitting into the front seat. I'm definitely bigger, she thought miserably.

Indiana University Hospital was located on a campus just west of Downtown Indianapolis. Just looking at the huge building intimidated Sandy. The surgeon was very businesslike and explained what the operation would entail. They would have to shave Sandy's head and cut into the top of her head to get to the tumor on her pituitary gland.

Recovery would take a couple of months, he said.

"Oh my," said Dora. Roseann reached over and patted her hand.

Sandy agreed to the surgery, "But not until after school's out. I want to graduate."

They set a date in early June, before Sandy's birthday on the 18th.

"Now," the surgeon said, "let's see how much you've grown."

Sandy took off her shoes and stood with her back to the wall. When the doctor stretched the tape measure up to the mark that was made at the top of Sandy's head, he let out a chuckle.

"You're now seven-feet-seven-and-a-quarter inches," he said. "You've broken your own record!"

42

John Kelly pulled a contract out of his briefcase and laid it on the table in front of Sandy.

"This is pretty exciting," he said. "At least it's something to consider."

"What is it?" Sandy looked skeptical. It was a week before her surgery and she didn't want to have to think too much. She had graduated from Shelbyville High with honors and that's all she cared about at the moment.

"The Guinness Museum of Records in Niagara Falls wants you to work at the museum starting in September. It would be a one-year contract, renewable if you want to stay another year."

"In New York?" Sandy frowned. She couldn't think of leaving home right now.

"The museum is on the Canadian side of the Falls, in Ontario," John explained.

"What would I have to do?"

"From what I understand, you would stand in front of a group of visitors with a microphone and tell them a little about yourself. Then they can ask questions or have their pictures taken with you. You'd be what they call a 'live attraction.'"

"That sounds like a sideshow," Sandy grumbled.

"Well, not quite. It's a really nice museum full of displays about world record-holders. There's even a life-size statue of Robert Wadlow, who was much taller than you are," said John.

"Yeah. I saw him in the *Guinness Book*," Sandy nodded. "How much does it pay?"

John cleared his throat. There was a twinkle in his eye.

"Forty thousand a year."

"Forty thousand DOLLARS?" Sandy's eyes grew big.

John nodded and smiled.

"Get out!"

"If you feel up to it after your surgery, it sounds like a really good deal. We could set you up in an apartment near the museum and we can negotiate other terms to make you comfortable," John advised her.

"Forty grand. Wow." She could do a lot with that kind of money, she thought.

"I'll leave a copy of the contract with you to look over," John said. "It could be a good opportunity for you."

"I'll think about it,'" said Sandy, "and let you know before my head gets whacked open."

43

Hamilton Street was so packed with people it was hard for Roseann's dad to find a parking place.

It seemed that half of Shelbyville was there to wish Sandy well on her trip to Canada and her new venture at the Guinness Museum of Records.

The doors of her van were open and suitcases were piled in the back. Sandy sat sideways in the driver's seat doing an interview with *The Shelbyville News*, wearing a new dark brown wig to cover up her hair, which was just starting to grow back after her 13-hour-long brain surgery two months earlier. Joey was across the street saying goodbye to his friends while Dora sat quietly in the back seat.

John Kelly, who was sharing the driving duties with Sandy, would fly home with Joey and Dora after helping Sandy get settled into her new apartment in Niagara Falls.

Violet stood on the sidewalk in front of the little yellow house with her arms folded, sulking. Obviously, she hadn't been invited along.

Roseann and her family got as close to the van as they could, hooking up with Julie and her mom. Her high school lunch buddies, Sarah and Mary Anne, also were there, as well as Allison Tanner, the former new girl in school who had become one of Roseann's good friends. Brenda Smart—who had gotten a vocal scholarship to the Juilliard School in New York—was on hand, too. Almost everyone had cameras.

The red-haired girl looked around her on this hot August morning, remembering the day two years earlier when her family moved to Shelbyville and how much she had hated it. She never thought she would fit in at Shelbyville High or have good friends like she did in Indianapolis.

She had been wrong. And she had learned so much from the people she had met in the Shelby County farming community. Even her pesky little brother, Scott, had thrived in their new town. He was going to miss Joey, whom he had taken under his wing from the first day the little boy and his big sister had visited his house.

Roseann looked over at Julie, who was grinning at her, a girl who was usually upbeat and funny despite her strained relationship with her dad. She had gotten a job at a local department store. Sarah waved at Roseann—she was going to be her roommate when they went off to college in a couple of weeks. And Mary Anne, sweet, starstruck Mary Anne, had gotten a job at a local bakery and was saving her money to go to California and get a job in the entertainment industry. Roseann loved them all.

Everyone should follow their dreams, Roseann thought. She had always known she wanted to be a writer. Sandy, who would have been happy working as a secretary, was moving to Canada to see if being the world's tallest woman was going to be a vocation or just a detour on her path of life.

Roseann looked over at the van. The news crew had finished their interview, and people were going up to Sandy to say goodbye. Joey came flying across the street and hugged all of the Bellamys before climbing into the van next to Granny.

Roseann waited until her family said goodbye to Sandy, then approached the van to give the tallest girl in the world her going-away gifts—a new backgammon game and a T-shirt that read "I like short people. I had three for lunch." Sandy cracked up when she saw it.

"I'm going to miss you," Roseann said.

"Me too. Knowing you has changed my life," Sandy replied, looking Roseann in the eye.

"And knowing you has changed mine." Roseann flung her arms around Sandy's neck. She didn't want to cry but felt tears stinging her eyes.

Sandy hugged Roseann, covering the girl's entire back with her large hands.

When Roseann pulled back, she saw that Sandy also had tears in her eyes. They both blinked, let the tears fall, and hugged again.

"Good luck with college," Sandy said, wiping her eyes.

"Thanks. And I hope everything goes well on your giantess gig."

They both laughed.

"I'll be home for the entire month of December, so maybe I can see you during your break from school," Sandy said.

"That would be awesome."

Roseann patted Sandy's hand and stepped away from the van to take a photo.

John jumped into the passenger seat and announced, "Let's get this show on the road!"

Sandy closed her door and started the engine, pulling away slowly from the curb while Joey waved excitedly from the back window.

Violet ran beside the van and shouted at Sandy.

"Be sure your brother has all of his things when he gets on the plane to come home," she yelled.

Sandy stopped the van and looked squarely at Violet on the sidewalk.

"He's not coming home. He's staying with me!"

Sandy smiled and drove off, while Violet stood on the sidewalk with her mouth hanging open.

"You can't do that!" she shouted, waving her fist toward the van.

"Did you see that?" Julie appeared at Roseann's side, looking at Violet and laughing.

Roseann nodded. Sandy must be savoring that last sentence, she thought.

Julie slipped her arm into Roseann's as they watched the van turn the corner.

"Thanks for being such a good friend these last two years," Roseann said to her.

"No big wazoo," she replied.

Websites of interest

www.sandyallensbook.com (To order Sandy Allen's biography and DVD *It's OK to be Different.*)

www.tall.org (Tall Clubs International)

www.7footersplus.blogspot.com (A list of the world's tallest giants and giantesses in history)

www.guinnessworldrecords.com (*Guinness Book of World Records*)

www.guinnessniagarafalls.com (Museum where Sandy worked)

www.shelbycs.org (Shelbyville Senior High School)

www.blueriverfoundation.com (contribute to Sandy Allen Memorial Fund online.)

Afterword

I came to know Sandy Allen in 1977 when I interviewed her for a magazine story. Over the years we became good friends, and she told me many stories about growing up in Shelbyville, Indiana, before becoming the World's Tallest Woman. What I discovered was that no one had written in depth about her struggles with the teasing she got about her size in high school which, along with a disruptive home life, made her situation even more difficult. I told her I wanted to put those years into a book, and she agreed. But there wasn't enough "story" there in the retelling of the incidents that happened to her, so to flesh it out I decided to write about her experiences as fiction based on fact. In this novelized version of Sandy's life, I have taken creative license with time elements, such as Sandy's getting her world record in high school instead of age 20, and having her pituitary tumor removed at an earlier age. In this book, Sandy is surrounded by fictional characters, some of whom are based on real-life people. Several of the places in Shelbyville are invented, others are real.

Sandy Allen passed away on Aug. 13, 2008, just two weeks after the manuscript for the book was finished. Fortunately, I was able to share the book with her a few days before she died and she was pleased with the story. My publishers and I set up a scholarship fund in Sandy's name that will benefit students at Shelbyville Senior High School. Sandy knew about the scholarship fund and was happy to leave a legacy to her hometown that went beyond being a world record-holder. To contribute, send your tax-deductible donations to: Blue River Community

Foundation, 54 W. Broadway St., Suite 1, Shelbyville, IN 46176. Put "Sandy Allen Memorial Fund" on your donation.

I would like to thank Art and Nancy Baxter of Hawthorne Publishing for their astute guidance—and patience with a first-time fiction writer—in making *World's Tallest Woman: The Giantess of Shelbyville High* a reality. I also am grateful to my friend, fellow author Mary Anne Barothy, for her support and input, for introducing me to the Baxters, and for showing me the art of networking. A huge bouquet of gratitude goes to Jackie Musgrave, who did the preliminary editing on the book and offered valuable suggestions. To Canadian girls Hailey Fitton and Courtney Eade, who love to read, many thanks for offering the critical wisdom of youth. Thanks also to Julie Wilhoit and Nyla Johnson for helping me to bring Shelbyville to life, to John Kleiman for use of photos, and to all of my other friends who encouraged me to write this story.

Most of all, I am thankful to Sandy Allen for showing me how a brave spirit and a great sense of humor can help anyone overcome adversity, and for giving me someone to look up to.

——Rita Rose